CLASS DYNAMICS OF AGRARIAN CHANGE

CLASS DYNAMICS OF AGRARIAN CHANGE

Henry Bernstein

AGRARIAN CHANGE AND PEASANT STUDIES SERIES

Fernwood Publishing
Halifax and Winnipeg

Kumarian Press
Sterling, VA

Copyright © 2010 Henry Bernstein

All rights reserved. No part of this book may be reproduced or transmitted in any form by any means without permission in writing from the publisher, except by a reviewer, who may quote brief passages in a review.

Cover design: John van der Woude
Printed and bound in Canada

Published in Canada by Fernwood Publishing
32 Oceanvista Lane, Black Point, Nova Scotia, B0J 1B0
and 748 Broadway Avenue, Winnipeg, MB R3G 0X3 www.fernwoodpublishing.ca
and in the United States by Kumarian Press
22883 Quicksilver Drive, Sterling, VA 20166-2012 www.kpbooks.com

Fernwood Publishing Company Limited gratefully acknowledges the financial support of the Government of Canada through the Canada Book Fund, the Canada Council for the Arts, the Nova Scotia Department of Tourism and Culture and the Province of Manitoba, through the Book Publishing Tax Credit, for our publishing program.

Library and Archives Canada Cataloguing in Publication

Bernstein, Henry
Class dynamics of agrarian change / Henry Bernstein.

(Agrarian change and peasant studies series)
Includes bibliographical references and index.
ISBN 978-1-55266-349-3

1. Agriculture--Economic aspects--Developing countries.
2. Agriculture--Social aspects--Developing countries. 3. Economic development--Social aspects--Developing countries. 4. Social classes--Economic aspects--Developing countries.
I. Title. II. Series: Agrarian change and peasant studies

HD1417.B376 2010   338.109172'4   C2010-902861-9

Library of Congress Cataloging-in-Publication Data

Bernstein, Henry.
Class dynamics of Agrarian change / Henry Bernstein.
    p. cm.
Includes bibliographical references and index.
ISBN 978-1-56549-356-8 (pbk. : alk. paper)
1. Rural development. 2. Social classes. 3. Capitalism. 4. Agricultural productivity.
I. Title.
HN49.C6B46 2010   307.1'412091724--dc22   2010018895

ISBN 978-1-55266-349-3 pb (Fernwood Publishing)
ISBN 978-1-56549-356-8 pb (Kumarian Press)
ISBN 978-1-56549-363-6 eb

Contents

ICAS Agrarian Change and Peasant Studies Series..*vii*
Acknowledgements..*x*
Preface..*xi*

Introduction: The Political Economy of Agrarian Change...................1
    The Big Picture: Farming and World Population....................1
    Who Are the Farmers Today?..2
    Marx's Political Economy 9
    Note...11

1   Production and Productivity 13
    Labour and Nature..13
    Divisions of Labour and Cooperation 16
    Reproduction 18
    Surplus, Exploitation and Accumulation 20
    Political Economy: Four Key Questions 22
    Notes..24

2   Origins and Early Development of Capitalism 25
    Defining Characteristics of Capitalism 25
    Origins of Capitalism #1: Paths of Agrarian Transition 27
    Origins of Capitalism #2:
    The Long March of Commercial Capitalism.......................32
    Theory and History: Complexities..35
    Notes..36

3   Colonialism and Capitalism... 39
    Phases of Colonialism 39
    Colonialism and Agrarian Change.......................................43
    Labour Regimes in Colonialism...53
    Notes..59

4   Farming and Agriculture, Local and Global 61
    From Farming to Agriculture...62
    "Nature's Metropolis" and the First
    International Food Regime (1870s–1914) 66

	From Free Trade to Protectionism (1914–1940s) 70
	The Second International Food Regime (1940s–1970s) 71
	Agricultural Modernization in the Moment
	of Developmentalism (1950s–1970s) 73
	Conclusion 76
	Notes 77
5	Neoliberal Globalization and World Agriculture 79
	Collapse of the Second International Food Regime 81
	Global Agriculture in the Moment of Neoliberalism 82
	The End of Developmentalism 84
	The End of the Peasantry? 85
	Notes 88
6	Capitalist Agriculture and Non-Capitalist Farmers? 89
	"Obstacles" to Capitalist Farming 89
	Exploitation: The Benefits of "Family Farming" to Capital? 92
	The Role of Resistance 95
	Conclusion 100
	Notes 100
7	Class Formation in the Countryside 101
	The Class Dynamics of "Family Farming" 102
	Classes of Labour 110
	Conclusion 112
	Notes 113
8	Complexities of Class 115
	Economic Sociology and Political Sociology 115
	Class Struggles in the Countryside 117
	"The People of the Land" 119
	Conclusion 122
	Note 123

Glossary *124*
References *131*
Index *139*

ICAS Agrarian Change and Peasant Studies Series

The Agrarian Change and Peasant Studies Series by the Initiatives in Critical Agrarian Studies (ICAS) contains 'state of the art small books on big issues' that each explain a specific development issue based on key questions. The questions include: What are the current issues and debates in the particular topic? Who are the key scholars/thinkers and policy practitioners? How have the positions emerged and developed over time? What are the possible future trajectories? What are the key reference materials? Why and how it is important for NGO professionals, social movement activists, official development aid and nongovernmental donor agencies, students, academics, researchers and policy experts to critically engage with the key points explained in the book? Each book combines theoretical and policy-oriented discussion with empirical examples from different national and local settings.

In the book series initiative, the overarching theme, 'agrarian change,' binds scholars, activists and development practitioners from diverse disciplines and from all parts of the world. 'Agrarian change' is meant in its broadest sense, referring to an agrarian-rural-agricultural world that is not de-linked from, but rather taken in the context of, other sectors and geographies: industrial and urban, among others. The focus is on contributing to our understanding of the dynamics of 'change'; meaning playing a role not only in (re)interpreting the agrarian world in various ways but also in changing it — with a clear bias for the working classes, for the poor. The agrarian world has been profoundly transformed by the contemporary process of neoliberal globalization, demanding new ways of understanding structural and institutional conditions, as well as new visions of how to change these.

The Initiatives in Critical Agrarian Studies is a worldwide *community* of like-minded scholars, development practitioners and activists who are working on agrarian issues. The ICAS is a *common ground*, a common space for critical scholars, development practitioners and movement activists. It is a pluralist initiative, allowing vibrant exchanges of views from different progressive ideological perspectives. The ICAS responds to the need for an initiative that builds and focuses on *linkages* — between academics, development policy practitioners and social movement activists; between the world's North and South, and South and South; between rural-agricultural and urban-industrial sectors; between experts and non-experts. The ICAS advocates for a *mutually reinforcing* co-production and *mutually beneficial* sharing of knowledge. The ICAS promotes *critical thinking*, which means that conventional assumptions are interrogated, popular propositions critically examined and new ways of questioning composed, proposed and pursued. The ICAS promotes *engaged research and scholarship*; this emphasizes research and scholarship that are both academically interesting and socially relevant, and further, implies taking the side of the poor.

The book series is financially supported by the Inter-Church Organization for Development Cooperation (ICCO), the Netherlands. The series editors are Saturnino M. Borras Jr., Max Spoor and Henry Veltmeyer. Titles in the series are available in multiple languages.

In memory of my parents, Esther and Harry

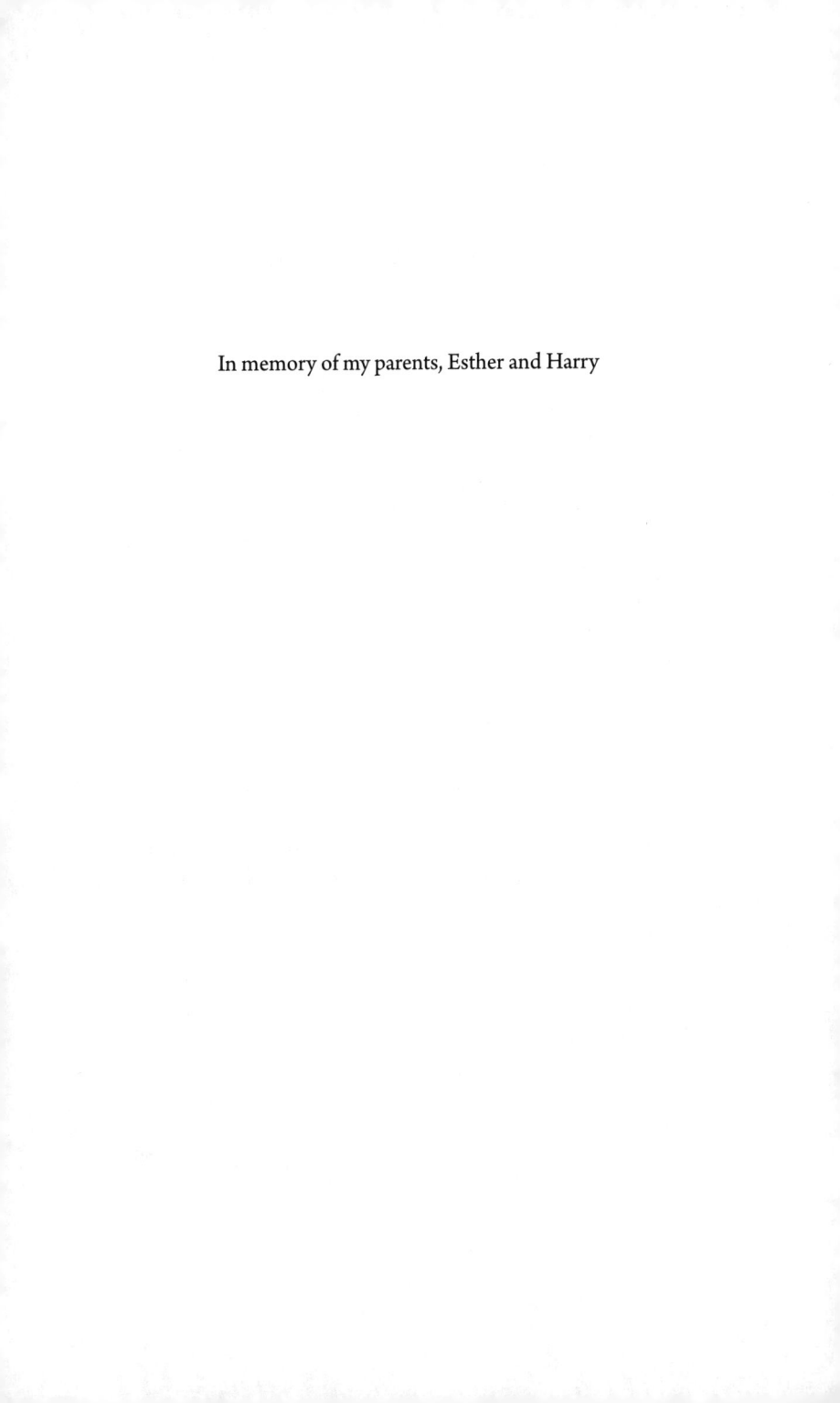

Acknowledgements

First, thanks to Saturnino M. Borras (Jun Borras) for his imagination and energy in establishing this new series of "little books on big ideas" concerning agrarian change, and for inviting me to write this first title for it. It will, I hope, contribute to productive debate between the books planned for the series.

I owe a major debt to my longstanding co-worker, Terence J. Byres (Terry Byres). He and I together edited the *Journal of Peasant Studies* from 1985-2000, and then started the *Journal of Agrarian Change* in 2001, both journals committed to the exploration of class dynamics in agrarian change historically and today.

This book draws on long periods of thinking about the issues it addresses, during which I have benefitted from the work of many others. I do not attempt to list them here; some, if not all, make an appearance in the text and in the list of references. In writing the book, I faced testing issues of selection, summary and style of presentation. The final result is certainly better than it would have been without the comments of comrades who read earlier drafts: Elena Baglioni, Jairus Banaji, Terry Byres, Jens Lerche, and Tony Weis. None will agree with everything here, for which I must take sole responsibility.

Preface

Class Dynamics of Agrarian Change by Henry Bernstein is the first volume in the Agrarian Change and Peasant Studies Series by ICAS (Initiatives in Critical Agrarian Studies). It is important to start the series with Henry's book for at least two reasons: the strategic importance of agrarian political economy analytical lenses in agrarian studies today and the world-class quality of the book. It sets the tone and raises the bar. It helps ensure that succeeding volumes will be as politically relevant and scientifically rigorous. A brief word about the series will put the current volume into perspective in relation to the ICAS intellectual and political project.

Today, global poverty remains significantly a rural phenomenon, with the rural poor comprising three-fourths of the world's poor. Thus, the challenge of ending global poverty, which is a multidimensional issue (economic, political, social, cultural, gender, environmental and so on), is closely linked to the resistance of working people in the countryside against the system that generates and continues to reproduce the conditions of rural poverty. While a focus on rural development thus remains critical to development thinking, this concern does not mean ignoring urban issues. The challenge is to understand better the linkages between these issues, partly because the pathways out of rural poverty paved by neoliberal policies and the efforts of mainstream international financial and development institutions to a large extent simply replace rural poverty with the urban form.

Many of the institutions (such as the World Bank) that propagate mainstream thinking on agrarian issues have the financial resources to dominate the research in this field and to produce and widely disseminate policy-oriented publications. Critical thinkers challenge this mainstream current in many ways, but their efforts are generally confined to academic circles, with limited popular reach and impact.

There remains a significant need of academics (teachers, scholars and students), social movement activists and development practitioners in the global South and the North for scientifically rigorous yet accessible, politically relevant, policy-oriented and affordable books in critical agrarian studies. In response to this need, the ICAS is launching the Agrarian Change and Peasant Studies Series. The idea is to publish state-of-the-art small books that will explain a specific development issue based on key questions: What are the current issues and debates in this particular topic, and who are the key scholars/thinkers and actual policy practitioners? How have such positions emerged and developed over time? What are the possible future trajectories, and the key reference materials? Why it is important for NGO professionals, social movement activists, official development aid and nongovernmental donor agencies, students, academics, researchers and policy experts to critically engage with the key points? Each book will combine theoretical and policy-oriented discussion with empirical examples from different national and local settings.

The Agrarian Change and Peasant Studies Series will be available in multiple languages, initially in at least three languages in addition to English: Chinese, Spanish and Portuguese. The Chinese edition is in partnership with the College of Humanities and Development of the China Agricultural University in Beijing, coordinated by Ye Jingzhong; the Spanish edition is coordinated by the PhD Programme in Development Studies at the Autonomous University of Zacatecas in Mexico, coordinated by Raúl Delgado Wise; and the Portuguese edition with the State University of Sao Paulo, Presidente Prudente (UNESP) in Brazil, coordinated by Bernardo Mançano Fernandes.

Given the context for and objectives of the Agrarian Change and Peasant Studies Series, we are pleased and honoured to have Henry Bernstein's book as the first in the series: it has a perfect fit in terms of theme, accessibility, relevance and rigour. We are excited and optimistic about the future of this series.

Saturnino M. Borras Jr., Max Spoor and Henry Veltmeyer
ICAS Editors
Agrarian Change and Peasant Studies Series

Introduction

The Political Economy of Agrarian Change

Agrarian political economy, as defined in the mission statement of the *Journal of Agrarian Change*, investigates "the social relations and dynamics of production and reproduction, property and power in agrarian formations and their processes of change, both historical and contemporary." Understanding agrarian change in the modern world centres on the analysis of capitalism and its development. By capitalism I mean a system of production and reproduction based in a fundamental social relation between capital and labour: capital exploits labour in its pursuit of profit and accumulation, while labour has to work for capital to obtain its means of subsistence. Beyond this initial and general definition, and indeed within it, there are many complexities and challenges that this book aims to explore and explain.

First, I want to set the scene, introduce my approach and identify key issues it addresses.

The Big Picture: Farming and World Population

Tony Weis (2007: 5) suggests that "the origins of the contemporary global food economy could be traced back through a series of revolutionary changes, which once took shape over the course of millennia, then over centuries, and which are now compressed into mere decades."

Millennia – From about 12,000 years ago, one form or another of settled farming became the material foundation of society. The reference to revolutionary changes taking place over millennia indicates that although changes were profound in their consequences they were typically gradual, more usually termed "evolutionary." Agrarian civilizations came to encompass most people in Asia, the "sown" areas of North Africa and Europe, and parts of the generally less populated expanses of sub-Saharan Africa and the Americas. In these agrarian societies the vast majority worked the land as peasant farmers. By 1750, they supported a world population of some 770 million.

Centuries – From the second half of the eighteenth century, the emergence and spread of industrialization started to create a new kind of world economy, to "accelerate history" and to transform farming. By 1950, world population had grown to 2.5 billion.

Decades – World population grew to six billion in 2000 (and is expected to increase to about nine billion by 2050). This suggests the part played by increases in the productivity of farming, which have kept up with population growth. And in 2008, global urban population equalled rural population for the first time, and started to overtake it.

One part of the big picture, then, is the growth in food production and in world population, especially since the 1950s. Both are aspects of the development of capitalism and of the world economy it created. Another part of that picture is massive global inequality in income and security of livelihood, and in quality of life and life expectancy, as well as in productivity. While more than enough is produced to feed the world's population adequately, many people go hungry much or all of the time.

Who Are the Farmers Today?

Some Figures

As countries industrialize, the proportion of their labour force working in agriculture declines. In 2000, the proportion of the total labour force employed in agriculture in the U.S. was 2.1 percent, in the European Union (E.U., then with fifteen member countries) 4.3 percent, in Japan 4.1 percent, and in Brazil and Mexico 16.5 percent and 21.5 percent respectively. In China, the proportion of the total labour force employed in agriculture has declined from about 71 percent in 1978 to less than 50 percent, which still amounts to over 400 million people. With an additional 260 million people in India and 200 million in Africa working in farming — in both cases about 60 percent of their "economically active population" — it is clear that the vast majority of the world's agrarian population today is in the Third World, or South.

This is corroborated by the standard estimate, derived from the FAO (Food and Agriculture Organization of the United Nations), that today "agriculture provides employment for 1.3 billion people worldwide, 97 percent of them in developing countries" (World Bank 2007: 77).[1] Some of those 1.3 billion qualify as "farmers," subject to many variations of what type of farmers they are, where, and *when*: during peak moments of the annual agricultural calendar? In good or bad rainfall years? Good or bad market years? In other words, not all farmers are farmers all the time. Many rural people may not qualify as "farmers" in any strong sense — perhaps a majority in some countrysides at some times and over time — because they lack land or other means to farm on their own account or are engaged in only "marginal" farming. Peter Hazell et al. (2007: 1) define marginal farming as "incapable of providing enough work or income to be the main livelihood of the household." They point out that in India, for example, the term is used for farms of less than one hectare, which make up 62 percent of all landholdings but occupy only 17 percent of all farmed land.

Terms and Concepts: Peasants and Small-scale Farmers

Terms like "peasant," "small" or "small-scale" farmer, and "family" farmer are often used interchangeably in ways that are easily confusing. This is not just a semantic issue but has important analytical issues and differences. The term "peasant" usually signifies household farming organized for simple reproduction, notably to supply its own food ("subsistence"). Often added to this basic definition are presumed qualities such as the solidarity, reciprocity and egalitarianism of the village and commitment to the values of a way of life based on household, community, kin and locale. Many definitions and uses of the term "peasants" (and "small-scale" and "family" farmers) have a strong normative element and purpose: "taking the part of peasants" (Williams 1976) against all the forces that have destroyed or undermined peasants in the making of the modern (capitalist) world. In my view, the terms "peasant" and "peasantry" are best restricted to analytical rather than normative uses and to two kinds of historical circumstances: pre-capitalist societies, populated by mostly small-scale family farmers (see Chapter 1) and processes of transition to capitalism (see Chapters 2 and 3).

With the development of capitalism, the social character of small-scale farming changes. First "peasants" become petty commodity producers, who have to produce their subsistence through integration into wider social divisions of labour and markets. This "commodification of subsistence" is a central dynamic of the development of capitalism, as explained in chapter 2. Second, petty commodity producers are subject to class differentiation. The historical framework of these processes is presented in Chapters 2 to 5, and its theoretical basis is explored further in Chapters 6 to 8. I suggest that as a result of class formation there is no single "class" of "peasants" or "family farmers" but rather differentiated classes of small-scale capitalist farmers, relatively successful petty commodity producers and wage labour.

Concerning size, some sources define "small farms" as those with less than 2 hectares of crop land, while others characterize small farms in the South by low levels of technology, reliance on family labour and a "subsistence" orientation (that is, "peasant"-like attributes). Thus, one criterion is spatial (farm size) and the other sociological (type of farming). The two criteria can diverge according to the conditions of farming:

> A 10-hectare farm in many parts of Latin America would be smaller than the national average, operated largely by family labour, and producing primarily for subsistence.... The same-sized holding in the irrigated lands of West Bengal, on the other hand, would be well above the average size for the region, would probably hire in much of the labour used, and would produce a significant surplus for sale. (Hazell et al. 2007: 1)

Finally, the term "family farm" often conflates farms that are family *owned*, family *managed* or worked with family *labour*. Some "family farms" combine all three characteristics, but others do not, as I explain further in Chapter 6.

Snapshots from the South

Beyond the statistical, definitional and conceptual issues noted so far, the following five quotations provide vignettes of farming in northern India, Bangladesh, Tanzania, Brazil and Ecuador.

> In the new capital-intensive agricultural strategy, introduced into the provinces in the late 1960s, the Congress government had the means to realize the imperial dream: progressive farming amongst the gentry. Within a year or two... virtually every district could field a fine crop of demonstration ex-*zamindars*... with their 30-, 40-, 50-, 100-acre holdings, their multiplication farms of the latest Mexican wheat and Philippines paddy, their tube wells gushing out 16,000 gallons an hour, much of it on highly profitable hire, their tractors, their godowns stacked with fertilizer, their cold-stores. (Whitcombe 1980: 179)

> Sharecropping is not much better. I do all the work, and then at harvest time Mahmud Haj takes half the crop. When I work for wages, at least I bring home rice every night, even if it's not enough. But when I work on my sharecropped land, I have to wait until the harvest. In the meantime I have no cow or plough. I have to rent them from a neighbour. The price is high — I plough the land for two days in return for one day's use of his cattle. In this country, a man's labour is worth half as much as the labour of a pair of cows! (Landless villager quoted in Hartmann and Boyce 1983: 163)

> Women weed the coffee, they pick coffee, pound it and spread it to dry. They pack and weight it. But when the crop gets a good price, the husband takes all the money. He gives each of his wives 200 shillings and climbs on the bus the next morning... most go to town and stay in a boarding house until they are broke. Then they return and attack their wives, saying "why haven't you weeded the coffee?" This is the big slavery. Work had no boundaries. It is endless. (Rural woman activist quoted in Mbilinyi 1990: 120–1)

The reason for all this was land speculation: two thousand hectares of virgin forest would be cleared, a thousand turned over to pasture, and then rubber tappers were deprived of their livelihood. From this developed the struggle for extractive resources in Amazonia, which is also a tribal area. The Indians... do not want private property in land, we want it to belong to the Union and rubber tappers to enjoy usufruct rights.... [In 1980] a very important leader, who headed all the movements in Amazonia, was murdered. The landowners... had him killed. Seven days later the workers took their revenge and murdered a landowner. This is the way justice operates. (Mendes 1992: 162, 168, interview published after Mendes' murder on December 22, 1988)

The *hacendado* moved to Guayaquil during the crisis. My father knew him well and he would rent us as much land as we wanted. The *hacendado* just wanted someone to watch his property until cacao came back. Javier and I had our little farm. We grew corn, beans, fruits. We even had a cow or two. But this was extremely hard. Sometimes there was nowhere to sell what we grew. And it was just my husband and I. We worked side by side in the fields. We didn't have children who could help out. And my family couldn't help much. The two of us had to do everything. We had few tools and no resources. And we didn't really own the land. So eventually I said let's follow Javier's brother Paco to Guayaquil. (Ecuadorean woman labour migrant quoted in Striffler 2004: 14–5)

The first vignette describes the wealth of rich farmers, who benefitted most from the Green Revolution in grain production in India, introduced by its Congress Party national government from the late 1960s. Elizabeth Whitcombe identifies those farmers as former *zamindars* or landowners, but they also included many rich peasants who had accumulated enough to become capitalist farmers (Byres 1981). They have highly capitalized farms and command substantial quantities of the "inputs" required to get the best yields from the new high-yielding varieties (HYVs) of wheat and rice seed introduced by the Green Revolution: tractors, irrigation pumps and fertilizer, stacked in their "godowns," or stores. The HYVs they use — and multiply themselves for future planting — originated in agricultural research stations in distant parts of the world. And the size of their farms would seem very big to most of their neighbours, and to nearly all farmers in Bangladesh or Tanzania, for example, but very small to their counterparts in Brazil.

The second vignette — that of a landless poor villager in Bangladesh — offers many contrasts with the first. It suggests a relentless daily struggle for a livelihood, with particular reference to that most basic need: securing enough to eat. The villager combines renting land, draft animals and a plough, to grow his own rice crop, with working for others for wages. Compared with the first vignette, this one does not provide any glimpses of places outside the immediate rural locale of the sharecropper. At the same time, the reference to working for wages might prompt us to ask who provides the labour on the thriving commercial grain farms of northern India described in the first vignette.

The third vignette, from Tanzania, provides a strong illustration of highly unequal gender relations (see Chapter 1). Unlike the previous two, it concerns an export crop produced for international markets, in this case by small farmers. We might want to ask how the land, labour and other resources devoted to growing coffee affect the cultivation of food for household consumption. Here, the payment after a good harvest, most likely the bulk of cash income for a year, is not used to meet the needs of the family but is spent on a "binge" by the male head of the household.

In the Brazilian vignette, we encounter themes long familiar in the agrarian histories of the modern world, including competition for land between different uses, and not least competition over forests — in this case between those who gain their livelihood from tapping rubber from wild rubber trees and those who want to clear forest to create pasture for large-scale ranching or to plant soy, which will be processed for animal feed. We also see a conflict over conceptions of property in land: between land as private property for the exclusive use of its owners and land as a common resource, to which particular communities or groups share usufruct rights, that is, common rights to use it. Moreover, as in so many countries formed from a colonial history, this conflict occurs between groups of people who are differentiated ethnically and culturally, as well as in terms of their power.

The final vignette describes the attempt of a young landless couple in Ecuador to make a go of modest farming on land rented from a *hacendado*, the owner of a *hacienda*, a relatively large estate in Latin America. The landowner had planted his land to cacao (cocoa) but abandoned it when the price declined drastically, the crisis that Maria refers to. Here, we have another international export crop — as in the case of Tanzanian coffee and Brazilian soy and beef — and also a glimpse of the difficulties of small-scale farming. Maria tells us that she and her husband Javier lacked enough labour between them to succeed, which raises questions about the kind of land they were farming and the tools they had to farm it. She also indicates that while they grew food for their own consumption, they also had to sell some of their crop because they needed money to purchase basic goods they did not produce themselves. While they were still young, they decided to follow Javier's brother Paco to see if they could earn a more secure livelihood in the large port city of Guayaquil, on Ecuador's Pacific coast.

These five vignettes point to the immense variety of types of farming and their social relations, of market conditions for crops, "inputs" and labour, and of environmental conditions of farming in different regions and for different types of people in the South. That variety makes any simple empirical generalization impossible. Nonetheless, in all their local and specific detail, these few vignettes give us glimpses of the following broader themes and dynamics of agrarian change:

- class and gender differentiation in the countryside;
- divisions of access to land, divisions of labour and divisions of the fruits of labour;
- property and livelihood, wealth and poverty;
- colonial legacies and the activities of states;
- paths of agrarian development and international markets (for technology and finance as well as agricultural commodities); and

- relations of power and inequality, their contestation and the violence often used to maintain them, from "domestic" (gendered) violence in Tanzania to organized class violence in Brazil.

The agrarian political economy, and the political economy of capitalism more broadly, used in this book to explore these broader themes and dynamics derives from the theoretical approach of Karl Marx.

Marx's Political Economy

Living in England from the 1850s to the 1870s, Marx (1818–1883) witnessed the transformations wrought by the world's first industrial revolution. In his great (and unfinished) theoretical work, *Capital*, Marx sought to identify the key relations and dynamics of the "capitalist mode of production" in its (then) most advanced industrial form. For Marx, capitalism — and especially industrial capitalism — is "world historical" in its nature and consequences. There was nothing natural or inevitable about its emergence as a new, and indeed revolutionary, mode of production, but once established its unique logic of exploitation and accumulation, competition and continuous development of productive capacity (Chapter 2), imposes itself on all parts of the world.

The fact that Marx analyzed the capitalist mode of production with reference to the industrial capitalism of northwest Europe leaves plenty of scope for different interpretations and debates about the histories of capitalism *before* modern industrialization and *since* his time, including

- how capitalism developed in primarily agrarian societies before industrialization (Chapters 2–3);
- how agrarian change has been shaped by industrial capitalism once it was established and spread (Chapters 3–5).

My goal is to use some of the concepts of Marx's theory of the capitalist mode of production to make sense of diverse and complex agrarian histories in the modern world. I propose some very general themes of the world-historical career of capitalism and try to connect them with the complex variations that particular histories weave from them (to borrow, from a different context, the formulation of the anthropologist Michael Gilsenan [1982: 51]). There is no suggestion that Marx provided everything we need to know about capitalism in theory or in terms of its histories, as he was the first to point out. Indeed the relation between his theoretical system (which is necessarily highly *abstract*, as well as incomplete) and its application in historical or *concrete* investigation remains a source of great tension and debate. In his notes on "The Method of Political Economy," Marx (1973: 101) suggested that "The concrete… is the concentration of many determinations" or what we might call, more loosely, "causal factors."

Each chapter in this book introduces theoretical ideas and questions and briefly illustrates them historically, sometimes through summary generalizations. Such generalizations, like those I use in Chapters 2 to 5 to outline the formation of the modern capitalist world, cannot do justice to historical specificities and variations. The same warning applies to the conventions of historical periodization: usually marked in centuries or part-centuries, periods are necessary to identify change, and we are unable to think about history without them, without asking what changed, how, why *and when*? At the same time, periodization runs the danger of obscuring the complexities of discontinuity and continuity. Historical periods in this book serve as "markers" of important changes: they do not signify that change from one period to another was always an encompassing, and dramatic, rupture with what existed before, although some historical processes involve more radical changes than others. With these necessary qualifications, the historical outline and sketches in this book are offered to illustrate an analytical approach that readers can test — that is, interrogate, apply, adapt or reject — for themselves.

To grasp that analytical approach and assess its usefulness is challenging. This is a challenging book, but how can understanding the world we inhabit, with all its complexity and contradictions, be simple? My aim is to provide some tools to think with, not to tell simple morality tales that we might find ideologically appealing (for example, "small is beautiful" versus "big is ugly," virtuous peasant versus vicious corporate agriculture).

Finally, the strongest arena of disagreement about Marx's ideas, and how to interpret and apply them, is among Marxists, or those strongly influenced by Marx. Those familiar with this history and its debates will no doubt recognize particular interpretations of materialist political economy that I present in this short book. But the book does not assume any prior knowledge of political economy, and I provide a glossary of key terms. An author's only hope is that readers will find enough that is relevant, interesting and provocative to reflect on and pursue further for themselves.

Note

1. Numbers of "small farmers" in the South are often exaggerated, sometimes greatly so, by those "taking the part of peasants" (see further below), for example, Joan Martinez-Alier (2002) and Samir Amin (2003), who give figures of two and three billion respectively.

Chapter 1

Production and Productivity

Labour and Nature

We presuppose labour in a form in which it is an exclusively human characteristic. A spider conducts operations which resemble those of the weaver, and a bee would put many a human architect to shame by the construction of its honeycomb cells. But what distinguishes the worst of architects from the best of bees, is that the architect builds the cell in his mind before he constructs it in wax. At the end of every labour process, a result emerges which had already been conceived by the worker at the beginning, hence already existed ideally. Man not only effects a change of form in the materials of nature, he also realizes his own purpose in these materials. (Marx 1976: 283–4)

An initial and general definition of "production" is the "process in which labour is applied in changing nature to satisfy the conditions of human life." As proposed by Marx, labour presupposes *agency*: the purpose, knowledge and skill, as well as energy, of the producer. In acting on natural environments, producers therefore modify the ecosystems they inhabit and indeed are part of.[1] Associated with production, and central to questions of human well-being — satisfying the conditions of human life — is the idea of *productivity*. Different concepts of productivity express the results of certain ways of doing things relative to other ways. Measures of productivity calculate the quantity of goods produced by the use of a given quantity of a particular resource.

In farming, one measure of productivity is land output or yield: the amount of a crop harvested from a given area of land.[2] Another measure of productivity concerns labour: the amount of a crop someone can produce with a given expenditure of effort, typically measured or averaged out in terms of time spent working, or labour time. Labour productivity depends to a great extent on the tools or technology the producer uses. For example, a farmer in the U.S. using a tractor and a combine harvester can produce a metric tonne (1000 kg) of grain, or grain equivalent, with much less expenditure of time and effort than a farmer in India using an ox-plough. In turn, the latter can produce a tonne of grain using less time and physical effort than a farmer in sub-Saharan Africa who cultivates with a hoe and other hand tools.

Alternatively, we can imagine how much producers using different kinds of tools produce on average over a certain period of time. In farming, a year is a relevant period because seasonality, according to weather conditions, is a key factor almost everywhere. We might find that in a year the African farmer produces one tonne of grain, the Indian farmer five tonnes and the American farmer 2000 tonnes. The Indian farmer's labour productivity is five times that of the African farmer, and the American farmer's labour productivity is four hundred times that of the Indian farmer and two thousand times that of the African farmer. These remarkable figures are suggested by French agronomists Marcel Mazoyer and Laurence Roudart (2006: 11), who also observe that the gap between the lowest and highest average labour productivities in the world's farming systems has increased massively since 1950 (see Chapters 4–5).[3]

Returning to my simple example, several further observations can be made. First, increases in labour productivity are associated with the application of other forms of energy than human muscle power: the animal energy of draught animals, the energy generated by the internal combustion engines of tractors and combine harvesters. Harnessing and applying other forms of energy, therefore, frees production and productivity from the limitations imposed by the energy of the human body alone. Second, it also allows a larger area of land to be cultivated relative to the numbers of those working on it. The area of land cultivated per farm worker in the U.S. has been calculated as fifty times the world average (Weis 2007: 83). Third, the productivity of farm labour is not just a matter of the forms of energy used in cultivation, but, like the productivity of land (yields), also reflects the quality of other "inputs": seeds, fertilizer, irrigation and so on. Finally, as farm labour productivity increases, smaller numbers of producers can supply food for greater numbers of people.

Different concepts and measures of productivity may come into conflict with each other; for example, in certain circumstances, yield in the sense of land output may be a more relevant measure than labour output. In the simple illustration above, average grain yields are significantly higher in the U.S. than in sub-Saharan Africa, although the difference in yield is much less than the extraordinary gap in labour productivity.

Other measures of productivity, like energy accounting, pioneered as long ago as the nineteenth century, and more recently atmospheric accounting, reflect concerns for the environment. Starting from the other end of the labour process — holding output rather than input constant — relative efficiency can be calculated by the units of energy (calories) used to produce a quantity of crops of a given energy or calorific value. In this instance, "low-input" farming, like hoe cultivation of grain, might be considered more efficient than "high-input" mechanized grain farming, even if it has lower yields and much lower productivity of labour (hence can feed many fewer people).

Additionally, we may want to calculate the implicit costs of the use of non-renewable resources — for example, the petroleum that fuels farm machinery — and the costs of pollution and other environmental damage (for example, soil erosion or degradation). These elements constitue what is now called the "ecological footprint" of particular types of production and consumption, in farming as in other economic activities.

So far I have illustrated one aspect of productivity — the tools and technology used in farming — and implied another aspect — the quality (as well as quantity) of human labour, that is, its command of the capacities demanded by certain kinds of tasks. If those capacities are not fully available, this affects the productivity of labour adversely: for example, a producer who lacks the skill to use tools effectively — whether hoe, ox-plough or tractor — or whose ability to perform arduous farm work in Africa or India is undermined by low levels of nutrition and health more generally, the effect of poverty. A third element has also been implied: the "raw materials" of farming, presented by different natural environments, which vary a great deal and can be managed more or less effectively — conserved, degraded or improved. Productivity also depends then on

- the fertility of soils, which can deteriorate or be maintained or improved through applications of organic or chemical fertilizers and different methods of cultivation;
- types and qualities of seeds, which may be improved; and
- the supply of water and its effective management, including dealing with the uncertainties of rainfall in non-irrigated farming.

The aspects of production and productivity noted so far concern some of the *technical conditions* of farming. But, as Marx remarked (1973: 86): "political economy is not technology." Farmers' activities involve them in relations with other people: whether in the labour processes of farming; whether the tools and materials they work with, including land they cultivate or graze their livestock on, belongs to them or to someone else; what sort of claim they have on the harvests their labour produces, and so on. These questions point us towards the *social conditions* of production: all the relations between people that shape how production is organized, including its technical conditions.

Divisions of Labour and Cooperation

We can assume that the three farmers in our simple example above did not make their own tools. This is perhaps obvious for the American farmer but is also a realistic assumption for the many farmers in India and Africa today who use factory-produced hoes and ploughs. Farmers have to obtain their tools from others, whose work is to produce those different kinds of tools. This is a simple example of the *social division of labour* between producers of different kinds of goods and services whose activities are complementary and who are related to each other through the exchange of their products. As the social division of labour increases in complexity, it makes available a more diverse range of goods and services across larger geographical spaces, which in turn presupposes effective means of transport and communication.

While we can assume that the three farmers are working on their own, this would not make sense in the case of the factories that produce the hoes, ploughs and tractors. Factory production requires a *technical division of labour*: the combination of different tasks performed by a number of workers to manufacture a single product. This suggests workers' *specialization* in different tasks, hence cooperation between them and coordination of their efforts, and an enlargement of the scale of production beyond what would be possible for single producers working separately. This makes possible a far higher productivity of labour than could be achieved, say, by an individual mechanic performing all the tasks necessary to produce a tractor.[4]

The greater the technical division of labour, the more complex cooperation it requires. Cooperation can also enhance the labour productivity of farmers using simple tools like hoes by enabling the following:

- economies of scale in the construction of common facilities (e.g., grain stores, water tanks);
- "complementation effects," that is, "adding individual labour to a process which only makes sense as a completed whole" (e.g., digging sections of an irrigation channel or building sections of a fence to protect crops); and
- timing effects, that is, concentrating effort to carry out tasks that have to be finished within a critical time (e.g., relating to seasonality in farming, like periods of rainfall) (von Freyhold 1979: 22–25).

The main points about technical divisions of labour and cooperation in these examples are that "the whole is greater than the sum of the parts" (what Marx termed "the collective worker"); technical divisions of labour and their effects for productivity require social organization; and what any single producer or worker does cannot be understood in isolation from the activities of others.

We have widened our understanding of the technical conditions of production as we have proceeded, especially with reference to agency, with which this chapter started. What Marx termed the "productive forces" includes not only technology and technical culture but people's capacity to organize themselves to make decisions about production, to carry them out and to innovate — all of which are shaped by the social conditions of production.

Reproduction

As indicated, the elements of the process of production themselves have to be produced. Even the land used in farming, while originally a "gift" of nature, is changed through people's interactions with it; for example, its fertility can deteriorate or be maintained or enriched. All those needs of constantly producing the conditions of farming, as of other human activities, are termed *reproduction*: reproduction of the means of production (land, tools, seeds, livestock), of current and future producers, and of the social relations between producers and between producers and others. For the moment, let us assume that all the needs of reproduction, securing the conditions of *future* production, have to be met from what is produced *now*. We can think of what is produced at any given time, say a harvest, in terms of the demands on it of various kinds of reproduction "funds."

I begin with the most obvious, the *consumption fund*: everybody has to eat to live, and the consumption fund refers to the immediate and daily need for food (as well as shelter, rest and other basics). Part of the harvest has to be allocated to the consumption of the producers and those who depend on them: children and those too old or unfit to farm.

Next I outline the *replacement fund*: tools used in cultivation become worn-out after a time; other "inputs" (or "instruments of labour," in Marx's term) tend to be used up more quickly, for example, seeds and fertilizers used up in each cycle of farm production. Therefore, part of current production has to be allocated to replace them. This can happen in a variety of ways, according to different social conditions. Throughout much of history, replacement was carried out within farming households: a certain proportion of the harvest was selected and saved as seed for the next cycle of cultivation; simple tools were made by farmers themselves or by neighbours who were specialized artisans (and who had to be compensated in some way for their work). In effect, satisfying the replacement fund represents a claim on labour and its product, whether keeping back part of the harvest for seed, using food stored from a previous harvest to feed people while they carry out tasks crucial to reproduction in-between farming seasons, acquiring basic means of production, and consumption, that farmers might not produce themselves.

Among the claims on the replacement fund, one is of distinctive significance: producing the next generation of producers, or what is called *generational reproduction*. What I have said so far has contained no reference to, nor used the prepositions of, *gender* — unlike Marx, in the quote above, who follows the old convention of "man" as a generic term for humanity and who assumes that the architect of his analogy is male (virtually all architects at his time were men). I signal gender now because bearing children — the first and necessary step in generational reproduction — is exclusively a female capacity, determined by biology. However, the exercise of that capacity is a social practice, shaped by social relations. While it is "ordained by nature" that only women can bear children, there is nothing "natural" about *whether* all women bear children, *when* they bear them, *how many* children they bear, nor, in some cultures, the pressure on women to bear sons. There is nothing "natural," apart from an initial period of breast-feeding, about the fact that the responsibility for bringing up children devolves on their mothers — or grandmothers, aunts, older sisters or female servants. Similarly, there is no "natural" or biological necessity that it is mostly women who carry out the tasks of maintaining the current generation of producers — cooking, cleaning, washing clothes, fetching water and collecting firewood — the activities of *domestic labour,* which are as vital to reproduction as any of the others considered here.

Domestic labour illustrates a further, and different, type of division of labour. We saw earlier one meaning of the division of labour as the specialization of productive activities between and within units of production. In the case of gender, specialization is established by the position that people occupy in particular structures of social relations. Gender relations — social relations between women and men, and the ideologies that shape them or justify them — provide the most widespread case of the social division of labour, although the particular forms of gender relations vary greatly across societies and groups within societies. They also change historically (which shows that they are not "fixed" by nature) and extend beyond the sphere of domestic labour to a range of other productive and reproductive activities, not least in farming systems, which exhibit a range of gendered divisions of labour.

Next is the *ceremonial fund*, which refers to the allocation of the products of labour to activities that create and recreate the cultures and social relations of farming communities (Wolf 1966), for example, rituals performed in preparation for cultivation and festivities after harvest. Other examples include celebrating rites of passage (e.g., birth, marriage), building a home for a new household, and marking the death of a community member (e.g., wakes, funerals).

Consumption, replacement and ceremonial funds all exist in societies centred on the "subsistence" needs and activities of their members and which may have little social differentiation other than gender and generation, e.g., the special authority of "elders." The fourth and final claim on the products of labour — the *fund of rent* — is a quite different arena of social relations.

Surplus, Exploitation and Accumulation

The replacement and ceremonial funds require a "surplus" product above what is required for immediate consumption. This is true of all societies, of which we can distinguish three broad categories in a kind of evolutionary sequence. The first is what we can properly term "subsistence" societies, which reproduced themselves at constant levels of consumption (and typically population size as well). This does not mean that those societies were "poor" in their own terms. Indeed, small groups of hunters and gatherers, or of those practising nomadic shifting cultivation (swidden farming), could often meet their limited needs with relatively little expenditure of labour time and effort — typically less time and effort than settled agriculture required (Sahlins 1972).

According to historian Colin Duncan (1996: 13), agriculture is "most usefully defined as the cultivating (or tilling) of soil marked out in fields," in contrast with "shifting cultivation" and nomadic pastoralism. Like many others, Duncan also observes that this "constituted a decisive break with previous modes of interaction between humankind and nature" (13). Settled agriculture emerged through human domestication of plants and animals and made possible a fund of rent and the historical emergence of a second category of society: agrarian *class* societies, whose development was charted in growing population size and density and in the formation of ruling classes, the state, cities and urban culture.

The fund of rent refers to payments farmers have to make to others. Those others might be landlords, who appropriate rent in kind (part of the farmers' crop), in labour or in money. Or they might be states, exacting payments as taxes in kind or money, or as labour conscripted for public works or military service; or religious authorities that are landlords or have the power to impose taxes or tithes. Or those others might be moneylenders or merchants, from whom farmers borrow against the value of their next harvest, as a money economy takes shape.[5]

In agrarian class societies, then, a "surplus" has to be produced above the needs of the producers for their consumption, replacement and ceremonial funds, in order to support dominant classes of non-producers. The capacity to *appropriate surplus labour* — labour beyond what producers expend on their own reproduction — signals social relations of *exploitation*.

The dominant or ruling classes of agrarian class societies consisted of royal dynasties, military and civilian aristocracies, religious and civil bureaucracies and merchant groups. Their consumption and reproduction — and those of the often large retinues that supported them (servants, soldiers, religious functionaries, clerks, court painters and poets — and architects!) — rested on the exploitation of producers, whether slaves, feudal serfs, other peasant farmers or artisans. Some of these societies — the famous agrarian civilizations of Asia and North Africa, Europe and Central America — experienced periods of expansion of territory and population. Those expansions were sometimes associated with innovations in the techniques and organization of farming and other productive activity, as well as of communications (e.g., the invention of writing), transport (especially water-borne transport), trade and military power.

While such ruling classes were concerned to regulate economic activity — the better to appropriate its surplus labour — and sometimes to stimulate it (e.g., by organizing the construction and maintenance of irrigation works), they did not attempt to "save" and reinvest the surplus product they appropriated to develop the productive capacities of their societies in any systematic way. Rather they were preoccupied with land and labour as the sources of their wealth (through rents, taxes, tribute), their power (supplying and supporting armies) and their glory (enabling them to consume luxuries, to build palaces, temples and churches, and to act as patrons of religion and the arts).

Exploitation of labour driven by the need to expand the scale of production and increase productivity in order to make profit — in short, *accumulation* — is a defining characteristic of the third category of society, namely capitalism. This is the subject of my next chapter, and indeed the rest of this book. Before moving on, I want to pull together some of the ideas and concepts of this chapter in terms of four key questions of political economy.

Political Economy: Four Key Questions

The following four key questions of political economy concern the social relations of production and reproduction.

Who owns what?
Who does what?
Who gets what?
What do they do with it?

1. Who Owns What?

The first question concerns the social relations of different "property" regimes: how the means of production and reproduction are distributed. "Ownership" and "property" have had different meanings in different kinds of society at different moments in history. The ideas and practices of *private* ownership and *private* property have been invented under capitalism and help to define it. This is particularly so in relation to *land,* the basis of farming. The widespread of conversion of land into private property — into a *commodity* — is one of the defining characteristics of capitalism.

2. Who Does What?

The second question is about social divisions of labour. Who performs what activities of social production and reproduction is structured by social relations between, for example, those who undertake specialized tasks within units of production; producers making different kinds of things; men and women; and the different classes in agrarian societies and in capitalist societies.

3. Who Gets What?

The third question is about the social division of the "fruits of labour," which is often termed the distribution of "income." As with ownership and property (above), that term does not just refer to income in the sense it has acquired in capitalism, namely individual or corporate money income. In forms of society before capitalism, and in some important areas of life under capitalism today, there are "fruits of labour" that do not take the form of money income. One example is food produced by small farmers for their own consumption; another example is the fruits of domestic and other unpaid labour.

4. What Do They Do With It?

The fourth question is about social relations of consumption, reproduction and accumulation. I have sketched this in terms of funds for consumption, replacement and ceremonial activities, found in all agrarian societies from the beginning, and for rent, which emerges with the formation of agrarian class societies. I have also noted, as unique to capitalism, the appropriation of surplus labour for purposes of productive accumulation. This final question is about how different social relations of production and reproduction determine the distribution and uses of the social product.

These four key questions can be usefully applied across different sites and scales of economic activity, from households to "communities" to regional, national and global economic formations. They can also be applied to different types of societies at different historical moments. There is also an implicit sequence in the four questions: social relations of property shape social divisions of labour, which shape social distributions of income, which in turn shape the uses of the social product for consumption and reproduction — which, in the case of capitalism, includes accumulation.

Notes

1. This last point is signalled in concepts of ecology made up of human and extra-human nature and their interactions.
2. For the sake of simplicity, I do not go into issues of plant or animal yield, although both have been central to processes of rising agricultural productivity, as indicated below. One measure of plant yield, of great interest to agrarian historians, is the ratio of crop harvested to seed planted.
3. That gap is reflected in shares of world trade in agricultural commodities today. Ten percent of the world's total agricultural production is traded internationally, of which the U.S. and E.U. each account for 17 percent, Canada, Australia and New Zealand combined account for 15 percent, and Brazil, Argentina, Chile and Uruguay together 13 percent. In short, 62 percent of world agricultural exports (by value) comes from countries with 15 percent of the world's population and just 4 percent of the world's agricultural labour force (Weis 2007: 21).
4. The situation in the earliest days of motor vehicles, before their mass production in large factories.
5. This represents a shift from the earlier assumption that all the needs of reproduction have to be met from what is produced now. Credit represents a claim on future production or income in order to satisfy current consumption and reproduction needs.

Chapter 2

Origins and Early Development of Capitalism

Defining Characteristics of Capitalism
The following three connected features contribute to the defining character of capitalism as a "mode of production."

Generalized Commodity Production
In capitalism commodity production is uniquely systematic and *generalized*. An ever increasing range of goods and services is produced as commodities for market exchange in order to make profit. Competition between capitalists drives innovation and productivity — a *systemic* development of the "productive forces" that is unique to capitalism (and also generates a tendency to over-production; see Chapter 4).

Imperative of Accumulation
Capitalism is distinguished by the central importance of *productive capital*. Productive capital invests in means of production (land, tools, machines, raw materials and so on) and labour power to work with those means of production, which it then organizes to make new commodities, creating new value as the necessary step towards realizing a profit on its investment. Marx expressed it like this: money (capital), or M, is invested in commodities (means of production and labour power), or C, in order to produce commodities with a greater money value, or M'; thus, M – C – M'. Profit is then reinvested to make more profit in an endless cycle of *accumulation* of further production and profit, what Marx called the *expanded reproduction of capital*. Capitalism is the only mode of production that presupposes that labour power and the means of production (not least land) are widely available as commodities.

The Commodity Labour Power

This brings us to the most distinctive feature of the capitalist mode of production, noted briefly in the Introduction: that it is founded on a *social relation* between capitalists, owners of the means of production, and workers, who exchange their their labour power, or capacity to work, in order to obtain their subsistence (means of reproduction). Labour power is fundamental because it is the only commodity whose use in production creates a greater value than its own value. In theoretical terms, this is because

- the value of labour power (like that of any commodity) represents the labour that has gone into producing it, expressed in the wage for which it exchanges; and
- labour power becomes the property of the capitalist who buys it and commands its use in producing new commodities of greater value.

Marx termed investment in labour power *variable* capital and investment in means of production (machinery, raw materials and so on) *constant* capital. The former is "variable" because only the application of "living" labour power can generate new value. The latter is "constant" because means of production can contribute only their existing value (as "dead" labour power, the result of previous production) to new commodities created. That difference between the value of variable capital (part of M in the simple formula above) and the value of the commodities generated by that investment (M') is *surplus value*, the specific form in which surplus labour is appropriated in capitalist production and the source of capitalist profit.[1]

Labour power has another unique quality: it is inseparable from the minds and bodies of its owners, who can combine in collective action to resist, moderate or overturn their condition of exploitation as sellers of their capacity to work.

Marx observed that workers in capitalism are "free" to exchange their labour power for wages with those who own means of production (capitalists). He was being ironic: workers in capitalism are legally free (unlike slaves, for example), but what if they "choose" not to exchange their labour power for wages? His point was that the legal and political compulsions binding labour, like slavery or serfdom in previous types of class society, are replaced in capitalism by "the dull compulsion of economic forces": sell your labour power or starve — you have the "choice"!

And Primitive Accumulation

Generalized commodity production, accumulation and the commodity of labour power did not emerge fully formed, suddenly, all at once and everywhere. Where and when they emerged, how and why, are much contested questions in debates about the origins and development of capitalism. A key concept in those debates is primitive accumulation: the processes through which pre-capitalist societies undergo transitions to capitalism. The social conditions of capitalist production, exploitation and accumulation had to be established initially by the means available to pre-capitalist societies. Consequently primitive accumulation is typically identified as "non-market" relations and dynamics, or "extra-economic coercion," as distinct from the market-derived compulsion of economic forces characteristic of developed capitalism.

Origins of Capitalism #1: Paths of Agrarian Transition
The English Path

For some scholars, modern capitalism emerged only with the industrial revolutions from the late eighteenth century onwards. Certainly, the advent of modern (factory-based) industrialization, and everything that goes with it, represents a decisive break with all previous history, which was that of principally agrarian societies. However, for other scholars, a *transition to capitalist farming* preceded, and made possible, the subsequent first industrial revolution in England. The origin of capitalism in this account occurred as a transition from feudalism in Europe, originally in England during the fifteenth and sixteenth centuries. Feudalism is based in the class relation between landed property and peasant labour, in which the "surplus" produced by peasants is appropriated by landlords through various forms of rent, as noted in Chapter 1. Peasants produced their subsistence on small farms, for which they paid rent or tribute to a feudal landowner, and might also have to work on the estate of the landlord, as a form of labour service or labour rent (see Table 3.1 in Chapter 3).

There was something of a general socioeconomic crisis in late medieval Europe (fourteen and fifteenth centuries), with different outcomes in its various feudal societies. England was the first where feudalism gradually gave way to a new agrarian class structure based in capitalist landed property, agrarian capital and landless labour. *Capitalist landed property* is different from landed property in pre-capitalist agrarian class societies because land now becomes a commodity in which its owners have private property rights; hence land is alienable: it can be bought and sold, rented or leased. This means that owners of capitalist landed property in the countryside do not necessarily farm it themselves (as capitalist farmers) but may rent it out to tenants who do.

Forms of tenancy in farming existed in agrarian societies before capitalism, and tenancy remains widespread in some regions of the Third World today, especially in Asia, like the example of the share-cropper in Bangladesh in the Introduction. In England's transition to agrarian capitalism, the striking feature was that tenant farmers represented an emergent *agrarian capital*, that is, they rented farmland on a commercial basis and *for commercial purposes*: to invest in commodity production in order to make profits and accumulate. In short, they were productive capital; hence the question arises: who provided the labour to work their rented farms?

This connects with the third and crucial class of agrarian capitalism: *landless labour*. "Landless" is an especially potent social marker in agrarian societies, of course. If you do not have land to work — whether accessed through use rights vested by membership of a farming community, through some form of tenancy or through clearing new frontiers for cultivation — then how will you secure your means of subsistence? A class of landless labour was formed through primitive accumulation as the dispossession of peasant farmers, a necessary condition of their *proletarianization*. In the English case, the mechanism of dispossession was the conversion of land to a commodity: its commodification (and renting to capitalist tenant farmers). The commodification of land included the enclosure of the commons: land used by peasant communities for grazing their livestock, collecting firewood, fishing and hunting, and other activities that provided a necessary complement to the subsistence they gained from cultivation.

While Marx was able to identify certain features of the emergence of capitalism that are of general significance, he did so on the basis of a particular historical experience, that of England. This is not surprising as his mature work was done there when Britain was the most advanced capitalist economy and in the full throes of the first industrial revolution. However, we should note that the "classic" case of agrarian transition in England might be regarded as exceptional precisely *because* it was the first such transition. In short, the English path does not necessarily provide a plausible general model of agrarian transition, in either its mechanisms (how it came about) or its particular form (the class trinity of capitalist landed property, agrarian capital and proletarianized labour). Several other well-known historical examples illustrate this point.

The Prussian and American Paths

Adding to Marx's English path of transition, Lenin (1870–1924) distinguished what he called the Prussian and American paths (Lenin 1964a). In the Prussian path, pre-capitalist feudal landed property transforms itself into capitalist commodity production, converting its previous labour force of peasants into dependent wage workers — and often also recruiting seasonal farm labour from poor rural regions elsewhere.[2] Lenin called it the Prussian path because it was exemplified by nineteenth-century eastern Germany (whose migrant farm workers came from Poland).

The American path was distinctive because agrarian capitalism in the northern and western U.S. did not emerge out of a transition from feudalism as in the Old World of Europe (and parts of colonial Latin America, see Chapter 3). In the American path, capitalist farming emerged from once-independent smallholders who become increasingly subject to the economic compulsions of commodity relations from the late eighteenth century (Post 1995). In these historical conditions, the class differentiation of initially small farmers is key — a theme introduced previously and explored in following chapters. For Lenin, the American path offered a more progressive prospect for Russia than the Prussian path, which was centred on an autocratic landowning-military class of feudal origin: the Prussian Junkers and their equivalents in Tsarist Russia.

The three paths outlined so far are summarized in Table 2.1, which draws on the seminal work of Terence J. Byres (1996).

East Asian Paths

Byres (1991) also drew attention to the distinctive agrarian contributions to capitalist industrialization in Japan and South Korea, summarized in Table 2.2. In these cases, there was no transition to agrarian capitalism like the English path with its dispossession of the peasantry through enclosure of land. What we have here is primitive accumulation for industrialization through what Preobrazhensky (1965: 85) described as "crushing taxation of the peasantry by the state *and transformation of part of the means so obtained into capital*" (my emphasis).[3]

These sketches of paths of transition give us an idea of historical variation and complexity, and their challenges to analysis. For instance, in the East Asian cases, peasant agriculture contributed part of its "surplus" to capitalist industrialization *without* a transition to agrarian capitalism as happened, in different ways, in the English, Prussian and American paths. This raises broader questions:

- Does the development of capitalism (always) require a transition to agrarian capitalism first (as in the English case)?
- Is there a wider range of possible connections between the development of capitalism and processes of agrarian change, in terms of the drivers of change and the forms of production on the land that they generate?
- Is the development of capitalism understood better, both theoretically and historically, in terms of different "national" paths (England, Prussia, the U.S., Japan, Korea) or in terms of the effects in different places at different times of the origins, as well as subsequent development, of capitalism as a "world system"?

Table 2.1 Paths of Agrarian Transition: England, Prussia, U.S.

	Peasants	Landlords	Form of production	Character of transition
English path 15c–18c	From serfs to tenants (14c, 15c); gradual differentiation of peasantry	From feudal lords to private landowners (16c–18c, including enclosures)	"Trinity" of capitalist landed property-capitalist farmers (including tenant farmers)-agricultural wage workers	Original transition to capitalist farming; special features included "improving" landlords willing to restrain rents to encourage investment in production —> "agricultural revolution" of 18c
Prussian path 16c–19c	abolition of serfdom 1807 (influenced by French Revolution)	Junkers (see above)	From some manorial production on landlords' estates (*Grundherrschaft*) to commercial estate economy (*Gutherrschaft*) with mostly tied wage labour (former serfs); from 1870s increasingly (migrant) wage labour	"Internal metamorphosis of feudalist landlord economy" (Lenin); or "capitalism from above"; contrast southern and western Germany: no *Junker* class, peasant differentiation —> emergence of capitalist farming "from below"
American path 19c	No feudalism; independent small farmers in North 17c–18c, slave plantations in South, 17c–19c	No large landed property except Southern plantations	Conversion of small independent farmers to petty commodity producers from late 18c; spread of (commercial) family farming from 1860s, especially with settlement west of Mississippi, supported by government; relative shortage of labour and high wage costs —> mechanization from 1870s	Petty commodity production "from below" in Northeast and through settlement of prairies; capitalist farming in California 19c; belated transition to larger-scale capitalist farming in South (mostly after 1945)

Table 2.2 Paths of Transition: East Asia

	Peasants	Landlords	Form of production	Character of transition
Japanese path 19c–20c	Tenancy central, and increased 1860s–1940	Mostly resident in countryside and with interest in improving farming	Tenant family farming (with extensive local industry and crafts), until post-1945 land reform —> owner cultivators	Primitive accumulation through taxation (versus dispossession) of peasantry; key role of state
South Korean path				
(a) Japanese colonial period (first half of 20c)	Tenancy central (as Japan)	Japanese (colonial) as well as indigenous	Extreme labour intensity on peasant farms subject to heavy rents and taxes	No transition in this period but some investment by colonial state (e.g., in irrigation) to boost rice and sugar production for export to Japan
(b) 1950s, 1960s Land reforms	Owner-cultivators	Owner-cultivators	Extreme labour intensity on family farms	State drives primitive accumulation for industrialization, facilitated by heavy taxation of the peasantry

Next I sketch an approach that gives answers to these and similar questions that are different from the approach of investigating particular "national" paths of transition to agrarian capitalism.

Origins of Capitalism #2: The Long March of Commercial Capitalism

This approach to the origins of and development of capitalism before modern industrialization centres on long histories of "commercial capitalism" — from the twelfth century onwards, according to some scholars or, more commonly, from the mid-fifteenth century. This approach is developed in explicitly Marxist terms in the work of Jairus Banaji (2010) and in a different fashion by Giovanni Arrighi (1994), who places more emphasis on cycles of financial accumulation and state formation and less emphasis on class relations of capital and labour. Jason Moore's ambitious project (Moore 2003, 2010a, 2010b) aims to account for this longer history of the development of capitalism in terms of the connections between patterns of accumulation, their increasingly extensive geography of "commodity frontiers" (in farming, forestry, mining, energy) and ecological change

Capital in Commercial Capitalism

The key actors in these long histories of commercial capitalism include classes of aristocratic (and later, colonial) landowners, who organized specialized commodity production on their estates (Banaji 1997), of merchants, who advanced credit and materials to handicraft and other producers of manufactured goods (Banaji 2007), of capital, in rapidly increasing extractive activities like mining and forestry (Moore 2003, 2010a), as well as classes of financiers, who funded much of this development, directly and indirectly, emphasized by Arrighi (1994; also Banaji 2007). All, it is claimed, were capitalists in a genuine sense: exploiting labour to generate profit; investing to expand the scale of production, often by increasing productivity; and developing and funding new sites and sources of commodity production and of markets for commodities.[4] And all this could occur before the emergence of modern industrial capital, and in many instances before, or independently of, the new types of agrarian capital and labour generated by the English path of transition.

Labour in Commercial Capitalism

Exploitation of labour, driven by the need to expand the scale of production in the pursuit of profit, serves as a useful summary definition of what capital in all its diverse forms, does. Is there a similarly concise definition that applies across the historically diverse forms of the labour that capital exploits? What is it that makes labour subject to "subsumption" by capital, in another term used by Marx, hence to exploitation?

I noted earlier the standard answer to this question: those who own nothing but their labour power, or capacity to work, (proletarians) have to sell it for wages with which to obtain their subsistence (means of reproduction). However, in transitions to capitalism, small farmers might lose their ability to reproduce themselves outside commodity relations and markets *without* necessarily being dispossessed of their land (and other means of production). Indeed, this dynamic of the *commodification of subsistence*, as Robert Brenner (2001) calls it, may provide a more generic basis of the subsumption of labour by capital than the outright dispossession usually suggested by notions of "proletarianization." In effect, the condition of "free" wage labour would thus represent only one form, albeit the most "advanced," of the commodification of subsistence.

Just as "commercial capitalism" can employ broader, and more flexible, notions of "capital" and "capitalist" than those usually associated with Marx's "capitalist mode of production," which he theorized in relation to industrial capitalism, the same applies to its conception of classes of labour. The crux of Banaji's argument is that capital is capable of exploiting labour through a wide range of social arrangements in different historical circumstances, including slavery in specialized commodity production on plantations. He is able to draw informative comparisons between labour regimes and labour processes on commercial landed estates, extending from late Roman Egypt through colonial Mexico and Peru to the *haciendas* of independent Latin America and the European settler farms of South Africa and colonial Kenya (Banaji 1997). Moreover, those comparisons demonstrate how fluid and ambiguous such categories as "landless labour," "tenant farmers" and "small peasants" often are in social reality, because the same people can move between those positions at different moments or even occupy them at the same time. The presumed boundaries between "free" and "unfree" labour can be similarly fluid and ambiguous. Even if "free" proletarian wage labour (as explained above) remains the most "advanced" form of labour in capitalism, and grows in relative weight as capitalism develops, it is not the only type of labour exploited by capital; nor, then, can it be uniquely definitive of the origins and development of capitalism.

"Paths" of Transition and the "World Historical" of Capitalism

Finally, it is striking that those who focus on these longer histories of "commercial capitalism" argue that capitalism was "world historical" in its very origins, that is, it necessarily involved international patterns of trade and finance. One good illustration of this is Arrighi's four successive "regimes of accumulation" in the history of the capitalist world system (Arrighi and Moore 2001): the Genoese-Iberian (fifteenth to early seventeenth century), the Dutch (late sixteenth to late eighteenth century), the British (mid-eighteenth to early twentieth century) and the American (from the late nineteenth century, with its hegemony, or dominance, eroding from the late twentieth century?). In this perspective, the original transition to agrarian capitalism in England occurred during a period of Dutch hegemony in world capitalism, while Britain became hegemonic only with its pioneering industrial revolution.[5]

Theory and History: Complexities

The discussion here reveals two contrasting conceptions of agrarian capitalism. One is based on a generalization of the original English path and its class structure of capitalist landed property and agrarian capital employing landless (proletarian) wage labour as uniquely definitive of agrarian capitalism. The other is expressed in Banaji's rejection of any single, uniform or "pure" agrarian capitalism and his suggestion that it is better "to think of agrarian capitalism as... based on the dispossession and control of labour by agrarian classes engaged in farming as a business" (2002: 115). He emphasizes that there are many concrete forms of dispossession and control of agrarian labour by capital in different historical circumstances: different trajectories of the subsumption of labour that connect with different trajectories of accumulation.

Another contentious issue — on which the two approaches diverge — is whether the abstractions formulated by Marx to theorize the industrial "capitalist mode of production" can, and should, be applied *retrospectively* in trying to understand the origins and early development of capitalism in primarily agrarian societies. Consider, for example, the following questions:

- How strictly should the distinction between capital invested in the production and in the circulation of commodities, typified in Marx's *Capital* as industrial and merchant capital respectively,

be applied to the histories of "commercial capitalism" *before* industrialization?
- How strictly should labour power, the basis of the appropriation of surplus value (exploitation) and hence capitalist profit, be limited to proletarians employed as "free" wage workers?
- How do we decide which of the great historical variety of specific forms of capital and labour are "capitalist" — integral elements of the origins and development of capitalism — or not? If not, are they "pre-capitalist" in some useful sense? Are they part of primitive accumulation? Alternatively, might they represent less and more "advanced" forms of capitalism in the different places and times of its development?
- Are less "advanced" forms of capital and labour in particular sectors and branches of a wider capitalist system, in particular places at particular times, connected with more "advanced" forms as an integral aspect of the extremely uneven development of capitalism on a global scale?

I touched on the first and second questions above. The third and fourth questions in particular indicate a movement from ideas and debates about the origins of capitalism to ideas and debates about the formation and functioning of a capitalist world economy. Central to the latter are the various phases of European colonialism from the sixteenth to twentieth centuries, what drove them, what forms they took, the kinds of agrarian change they induced and with what consequences — the subject of Chapter 3. We shall see that interpretations of these world-historical dynamics are shaped, in some important respects, by the kinds of issues noted here concerning alternative approaches to the origins of capitalism.

Notes

1. The *rate of surplus value* is the ratio of new value to the value of variable capital invested in producing it, while the *rate of profit* is the ratio of new value to the value of the variable *and* constant capital invested in producing it.
2. This is a pattern familiar from many countrysides of the South, and indeed the North today: West Africans and North Africans in south-

ern Europe; East and Central Europeans in northern Europe; Latin Americans in the U.S.
3. Of course, the story was more complicated as all historical processes are; while subjected to increased taxation during the nineteenth and early twentieth centuries, Japanese farmers — encouraged by landlords and the state — also increased rice yields substantially and generated a range of dynamic local industries using agricultural materials (Francks 2006).
4. Moore (2010a) suggests key developments of the productive forces in the century after 1450 in silver mining, sugar production, forestry, iron making and ship building. Note, however, that this list does not include grain farming.
5. Note that the Netherlands ran England very close for the distinction of the first transition to agrarian capitalism — although, once more, along a somewhat different path — as well as in its early capitalist industrialization. Arrighi's schema suggests a shift in centres of economic power in the global development of capitalism from southern to northern Europe and from Mediterranean- to Atlantic-oriented trade and finance.

Chapter 3

Colonialism and Capitalism

The histories of when and how capitalism developed as a world system, and in the different regions of the modern world, are diverse and complex. In this chapter I can only sketch a central element in the formation of the modern world: the different types of colonialism imposed on Latin America, Asia and Africa at different times, and some of their effects.

Phases of Colonialism
Feudalism and Commercial Capitalism
(Sixteenth Century)
The motivations, forms and cumulative intensity of the "expansion of Europe" through colonialism were initially driven by its linked crises of feudalism and the development of commercial capitalism (Chapter 2). In the sixteenth century, colonial rule was first imposed in the Caribbean and parts of Latin America, where the aftermath of Spanish conquest had devastating demographic and ecological effects. The quest for treasure that first spurred exploration of a western route from Europe to the Indies led to the opening of the great silver mines of Peru and later Mexico, absorbing massive amounts of usually forced labour from indigenous populations. The domestic economies and overseas trade of Spain and Portugal, which colonized Brazil, were to face increasing competition from England and Holland in particular, small countries in northwest Europe that were moving more rapidly towards agrarian and subsequently industrial capitalism (Chapter 2).

Merchants, Slaves and Plantations
(Seventeenth and Eighteenth Centuries)
In the course of the seventeenth century, new forms of colonial settlement, production and trade were exemplified by British interests in North America and British and Dutch activity in the Caribbean. The

Virginia colony in British North America established a plantation economy based first on indentured labour from Europe and then on slave labour from Africa. Tobacco and cotton exports from its American colonies, and sugar from its Caribbean colonies, were to become more important to the British economy, especially to its emerging class of manufacturers, than the luxury spices and silks of the Asian trade. In short, British colonization of North America and the Caribbean initiated a new kind of international trade linking large-scale production of raw materials in the colonies for manufacturing in Europe, the procurement from Africa of slave labour for plantation production, and the development of markets for European goods in the colonies. The first major destination of the African slave trade was the sugar plantations of coastal Brazil. The Dutch played a leading role in the spread of slave production to the mainland coasts and islands of the Caribbean, to meet the demand by merchants and sugar refiners in Holland, while the British developed the slave plantation system of what is now the southern U.S.

For all these important moments in colonization and their connections with trajectories of accumulation in Europe, the second half of the seventeenth century was a period of relative decline in Europe's international trade and the fortunes of its overseas merchant companies. This was connected with turbulent events in Europe, including a significant new type of mercantilist trade war, conducted principally at sea by armed fleets.

The eighteenth century saw a revival and intensification of European expansion. There was a major growth in the Atlantic slave trade from West Africa, and European adventurers and merchants extended their exploration, pillage and pursuit of commercial advantage along the coasts of Africa and within Asia. These activities continued and developed the forms of expansion begun in the sixteenth century, marked by armed conflicts between Europeans as well as between them and the peoples of the areas on which they sought to impose their domination. The British defeated the French for control of India and Canada — instances that demonstrate how widespread were the regions of European colonial expansion, and contestation, by the mid-eighteenth century.

In sum, in the course of the seventeenth and eighteenth centuries, the "expansion of Europe" intensified and a recognizable international division of labour was established. Most colonization was undertaken by merchant companies rather than by European states themselves, with the notable exceptions of Spain and Portugal in Latin America. At the same time, of course, European states supported their merchants — like the British East India Company and the Dutch East India Company — through political, diplomatic and military, above all naval, means.

Industrial Capitalism and Modern Imperialism (Nineteenth and Twentieth Centuries)

During the nineteenth century, the capitalist world economy was increasingly shaped by industrialization, with a turning point in the 1870s and the beginning of the "second industrial revolution" (see Chapter 4). This generated demand for ever-increasing quantities of tropical agricultural commodities for processing and manufacturing, as well as for minerals from colonial mines. From the 1870s, the world experienced increasing overseas investment in colonial extractive sectors (plantation and peasant agriculture, mining) and their transport links to world markets (railways, shipping); the final great wave of colonial expansion (in sub-Saharan Africa, Southeast and Western Asia), now undertaken by European states rather than by merchant companies; increasing exposure of British industry, partly cushioned by Empire, to competition from the rapidly industrializing economies of Germany and the U.S.; and the emergence of Japan as the first non-western industrial power.

Africa exemplified the speed of the last wave of colonial expansion. In 1876, European powers ruled about 10 percent of Africa, primarily its northern regions bordering the Mediterranean and the colonies of what later became South Africa. By 1900, they had extended their domination to 90 percent of the continent. The "scramble for Africa," formalized by the conference of Berlin in 1884–5, occurred during the first major manifestation of the cycles of boom followed by slump of the new world economy of industrial capitalism, namely the great depression of late nineteenth-century Europe (1873–96), itself followed by the "golden age" of 1896–1914.

For Lenin (1964b), the great depression of the late nineteenth century marked a critical turning point from an earlier "competitive" stage of capitalism to what he called monopoly capitalism or imperialism, characterized by the concentration of capital in the form of large industrial corporations closely linked with banks. "Monopoly" does not mean that competition ceased to exist but that it took more extreme and dangerous forms, leading to the First World War in 1914, which was the immediate stimulus to Lenin's theory of imperialism. Lenin suggested that European colonial expansion by the late nineteenth century, unlike earlier waves of colonization, was driven by the need to find new outlets for the *export* of capital, for two reasons. One was the dynamic of constantly accelerating accumulation, for which industrial capitalism needed increasing sources of raw materials and ever larger markets for its manufactured goods. The second was the search for overseas investment opportunities as intense competition in Europe depressed capital's rate of profit.

Lenin's theory of imperialism has been criticized on analytical, empirical and ideological grounds. One criticism is that two of the principal elements of imperialism he identified were typified by European countries with very different paths of capitalist development and with colonial possessions on vastly different scales. On one hand, Britain exemplified capital export and had by far the largest colonial empire, although much more of its overseas investment went to countries of European settlement in the Americas than to its colonies in Asia and Africa. On the other, Germany at that time best exemplified the combination and concentration of giant industrial corporations and banks, what Lenin (following Hilferding, 1981) called "finance capital," and had few colonial territories. Another criticism is that Lenin overstated the processes he identified, which can be seen more clearly in today's "globalization" than in the early twentieth century.[1]

While Lenin sought to connect the economic downturn of late nineteenth-century Europe with the emergence of modern imperialism and the last great wave of capitalist colonization, part of the continuing interest in his theory is that imperialism, in his sense, does not depend on colonies. In the world of 1916, he illustrated this in relation to Argentina, a politically independent country (populated mostly by European immigration) that he described as a "semi-colony" of British capital, and in relation to Portugal, as a kind of client state of Britain at the same time as it was a minor league colonial power in Africa and Asia (having lost Brazil, the former jewel in its imperial crown).

Imperialism as the distinctive international form of modern capitalism thus has a different meaning than the usual sense of "empire" as a political entity, for which the British colonial empire was simply one of many examples, like the Roman Empire or the great historical empires of West, South and East Asia. Lenin was clear that modern imperialism would survive the end of colonialism. Moreover, it is possible to argue that imperialism as a fully capitalist world economy could only be completed with independence from colonialism in Asia and Africa, making way for the "dull compulsion of economic forces," both internationally and domestically, to replace the political and legal coercions of colonial rule (Wood 2003).

I have more to say about the period since the end of colonial empire in Chapters 4 and 5. Next, I want to elaborate briefly this overview of capitalism and colonialism, to sketch how colonialism affected the lives of people in agrarian societies subjected to it, with particular attention to their labour and land.

Colonialism and Agrarian Change

The colonial project depended on making the colonies "pay their way" and generate profits for colonial powers. This meant controlling the labour of the colonial subjects of agrarian societies, which required intervening in their institutions and practices of land allocation and use, sometimes destroying them, sometimes modifying them. The making of colonial economies involved the breaking of pre-colonial modes of peasant subsistence and of rent (in agrarian class societies). Here I can only illustrate some of the ways that colonial powers attempted to restructure the different kinds of agrarian relations they encountered in different places at different times, and some of the effects (unintended as well as intended) of how they did so.

Latin America and the Caribbean

The earliest colonial agrarian change occurred in the Caribbean, Latin America and North America: the principal regions of slave production in the emergent capitalist world economy, from the sugar plantations of Portuguese Brazil and subsequently of the British and French Caribbean, to the cotton and tobacco plantations of the southern colonies of British North America. At the moment of colonial conquest these New World plantation zones were relatively lightly populated by mostly "subsistence" societies. The forcible dispossession of indigenous peoples to secure land was accomplished relatively easily, and colonial planters resolved the problem of labour supply by importing slaves. Slavery was finally abolished in the British Empire in 1833, and continued until 1865, 1888 and 1889 in the U.S., Brazil and Cuba respectively.

In most of Spanish America, another form of landed property dominated the economic life of the countryside and much of its social, political and cultural life from the late seventeenth century, namely the *hacienda*, or landed estate. The *hacienda* system adapted the feudal institutions and practices familiar to Spanish colonists. It combined granting settlers rights to levy tribute on indigenous communities in the form of goods or labour services (*encomienda*) and rights to land (*mercedes de tierras*), originally given for military service to the Spanish Crown. Combining land and labour in the *hacienda* created a type of landed property structurally very similar to the manor of European feudalism, including its two basic forms of organizing farming, as shown in Table 3.1 (based on Kay 1974).

Securing control of rural labour depended on expropriating and enclosing land, in order to undermine the access of indigenous farmers to their means of subsistence. The extension of the different forms of the *hacienda* system reflected several factors. Its initial formation and extension involved protracted struggles, especially in areas with higher population densities and strong peasant communities, such as parts of Central America and the Andean highlands. In more sparsely populated areas like the plains of Argentina, Uruguay and Chile, *hacienda* formation came later and more swiftly, with labour supply met more through immigration.

Table 3.1 Two Types of Hacienda

Land use	Labour regime	Form of surplus appropriation
A. Multi-farm estate (principally peasant farms)	Peasant cultivation of land allocated to them, and control of the labour process	Rent in kind, rent in money, crop shares
B. Landlord estate (landlord's farm plus peasant "subsistence" plots or *minifundia*)	Peasants work increasingly on landlord's (enlarged) farm while maintaining their subsistence plots	Labour rent (=unpaid labour on landlord's farm)

Another key factor expressed time as well as place. Struggles between colonial landlords and indigenous peasants were also affected by historical patterns of the commercialization of agriculture in the developing and fluctuating world market. As the potential profitability of farming increased with rising market demand, landowners sought to enlarge their own farms and to force more labour from their *hacienda* tenants, thus converting rent in kind or money to labour rent. When landlords confronted a shortage of labour for their own commercial farming *and* lacked the ability to resolve this through coercive means, they might have to pay tenants for their work, at least in part, which suggests a transition from labour rent to wage labour (as happened along various paths of transition in Europe).

There is much debate among historians about where, how much and *when* practices of debt bondage were instrumental in recruiting labour for large commercial estates. Debt bondage is an arrangement in which those who are indebted, typically small farmers and landless rural labourers, have to work off their debt for the creditor — a landowner, richer farmer, merchant or, quite commonly in Asia, a third party who buys or "rents" the debt. Some scholars argue that transitions to wage labour in Latin America started relatively early (from the seventeenth century in some regions of commercial *hacienda* production), even if it was often and for long periods also marked by elements of debt bondage and other constraints on the "freedom" of wage labour. This touches on issues of characterizing agricultural labour, noted in Chapter 2 and which I come back to at the end of this chapter.

Most of Latin America became independent of colonial rule in the first half of the nineteenth century (before most of Africa was colonized) with a legacy of widespread dispossession of land and its concentration in *haciendas*; the restriction of most indigenous farming to sub-subsistence holdings called *minifundios*, by contrast with the extensive *latifundios*, in effect another name for *hacienda*; and widespread rural wage labour, often combined with marginal farming and elements of debt bondage and state coercion.

Latin America entered a new agricultural export boom from the 1870s to 1920s, involving the extension and intensification of *hacienda* production, from the tropical and sub-tropical areas of Central America to extensive grain and cattle farming in the prairies of Uruguay, Argentina and Chile. In the lowlands of southern Mexico the

> combination of strong markets for tropical exports (sisal, rubber, sugar), a labour shortage, geographical isolation, and a... state willing to support the planters with force explains the virtual enslavement of masses of Mayas and Yaquis... in Mexico beginning in the 1870s, in Guatemala where the reduction of Indian lands was accompanied by anti-vagrancy laws, in Bolivia where two-thirds of the rural population became dependent on haciendas, and in fact throughout the Andean spine, the resources and means of independent livelihood of a great many rural people were reduced. (Bauer 1979: 37, 52)

Some labour shortages were resolved through immigration. Between 1847 and 1874, over a quarter of a million Chinese indentured workers toiled in the plantations of Cuba and coastal Peru. In Brazil, with the end of slavery, coffee planters got the government to subsidize the costs of mass immigration from Europe. From 1884 to 1914, some 900,000 European immigrants arrived in Sao Paulo, mostly to work in the coffee estates (Stolcke and Hall 1983).

Latin America today has perhaps the greatest range of forms of agrarian social relations and farming anywhere in the world. On one hand, there are relatively fewer people in agricultural employment than in other major regions of the South. Brazil has an extraordinary concentration of modern agribusiness capital, and technical and financial expertise, with the potential to become the largest agricultural export economy in the world, while the "southern cone" countries of Argentina, Uruguay and Chile are also major agricultural exporters with highly capitalized and specialized branches of farming. On the other hand, there are instances of resilient or resurgent "peasant" (*campesino*) identity in areas of more concentrated indigenous populations in Central America and the Andes, and further south in zones of small-scale settler farming. Struggles over land and the contemporary conditions of farming have generated some of today's best-known rural social movements, like La Vía Campesina ("the peasant way") in Central America and the Movimento dos Trabalhadores Rurais Sem Terra (MST, or Landless Workers Movement) in Brazil.

South Asia

British expansion in the eighteenth century into the interior of South Asia, with its many populous areas of peasant farming, eventually created the largest colonial possession of all, the "jewel in the crown" of Britain's colonial empire. Plunder gradually gave way in the nineteenth century to considerations of more systematic sources of revenue and profit: a transition from piracy to bureaucracy, as Barrington Moore (1966: 342) characterized it in relation to the two main land revenue systems of colonial India.

The first stemmed from the Permanent Settlement of Bengal and adjacent areas in northern India from 1793, in which the *zamindars* (whose descendants we encountered in the first vignette in the Introduction) were transformed from the tax-farmers and revenue collectors of the previous Mughal state into landlords with certain property rights in land. The colonial authors of the Settlement hoped that the *zamindars* would thereby become a solid class of bourgeois property and replicate Britain's agrarian capitalism. For various reasons, this ambition was not realized (like many imperial fantasies). *Zamindar* power varied widely across the diverse countrysides of the Raj (with its sub-continental scale), as a result of the struggles of *zamindars* with castes of cultivators on one hand and with classes of moneylending and merchant capital on the other.

The Bengal land settlement, as well as the eventual incorporation of 600 or so princely states in the British Raj (colonial state, literally "reign" in Hindi) was also a means of trying to secure indigenous political allies in administering these vast colonial domains. This was one example of a more general practice of colonial "complicity with older [pre-colonial] structures of power" (Bagchi 2009: 87), also applied earlier by the Spanish in Latin America in the office of *cacique* (native king, chief or headman) and later in Africa through "indirect rule," which incorporated chiefs and headmen in the lower levels of the colonial administrative hierarchy to maintain order in the countryside, organize tax collection and mobilize labour.

The other major land "settlement" was the *ryotwari* system (after *ryot* or peasant), introduced further south in large parts of Bombay and Madras. This confirmed property rights in land, at least in principle, on those cultivating it, subject to annual payment of a money tax. Barrington Moore (1966: 344) concludes:

> The [land] settlements were the starting point of a whole process of rural change whereby the imposition of law and order and associated rights of property greatly intensified the problem of parasitic landlordism. More significantly still, they formed the basis of a political and economic system in which the foreigner, the landlord, and the moneylender took the economic surplus away from the peasantry, failed to invest it in industrial growth and thus ruled out the possibility of repeating Japan's way of entering the modern era.

Moore's point was that the land systems generally made it more lucrative to extract rent from tenant peasantries who worked it than to invest in raising agricultural production and productivity, thus "parasitic" rather than productive landlordism.[2]

The British Raj, however, was not a settler colonialism as in British North America and Latin America. There was no expropriation of land on a significant scale to accommodate European settlers, although there were some plantations for export crops. The largest single area of land enclosed was under the control of the colonial government's Forestry Department, much of it given over to commercial timber exploitation; the removal of forest from the commons available to peasant farmers, pastoralists and "tribal" people reduced the resources they could draw on for their subsistence activities. At the same time, peasants were increasingly integrated into the international capitalist economy by means of "forced commercialization," in the term of Krishna Bharadwaj (1985). They had increasing money obligations to meet; they produced export commodities like cotton, jute and opium (traded with China to pay for tea destined for British consumption) as well as food for both domestic and export markets; and their rents and taxes supported not only indigenous landowners, merchants and moneylenders but also the profits of British trading houses and the revenues of the colonial administration and the British imperial state.

For most peasant farmers, "forced commercialization" and the commodification of subsistence more broadly did not generate major increases in agricultural output, let alone productivity. The exactions of the "fund of rent" poorer peasants had to bear, their indebtedness, and the resulting diversion of resources from food production for their own consumption, made their own contributions to the image of India, and China, as countries especially vulnerable to famine. While famine was associated with extreme weather conditions, it is notable that India continued to export food during major famines in the late nineteenth century and again in 1943–44 in Bengal (Sen 1981). The capacity of many Indian peasants to deal with the consequences of adverse weather and poor harvests had been undermined by the commodification of subsistence, the demands of colonial taxation and the economic ideology of the colonial administration (Davis 2001).

Note also that the import of factory-produced goods, like cotton textiles, from Britain, undermined indigenous manufacturing and handicrafts, which were important to diversified rural economies. Amiya Bagchi (2009) suggests that the impact of colonialism in the nineteenth century was to increase the "ruralization" and "peasantization" of India, as well as to increase poverty, and that imperialist penetration of China had a similar effect even without direct colonial rule.

However, the development of commodity production also stimulated class differentiation among farmers in India as elsewhere (in India often following existing lines of caste inequality). Banaji (2002: 114) concludes:

> The rapid commercial expansion of the nineteenth century was bound up with a kind of capitalism rooted in the growing dominance of upper and middle castes of substantial cultivators. They accounted for the widespread employment of permanent farm servants [labourers], dominated the local credit markets... and came increasingly to control the land market where this had evolved.

He also notes that the development of this "kind of capitalism" varied across the diverse countrysides of the Raj, as did the strength of "substantial cultivators" relative to landlords and moneylenders and their claims on the agricultural surplus.

Sub-Saharan Africa

Systematic colonization of sub-Saharan Africa from the late nineteenth century produced three "macro-regions," identified by Samir Amin (1976) as the *économie de traite* (roughly "trade economy"), labour reserves and concessionary companies. The first was characterized by export production by peasant farmers, and in some cases by larger-scale indigenous producers, and typically organized by metropolitan trading houses. As in India, the *économie de traite* did not entail widespread land expropriation and peasant dispossession. Its commodification of rural economy proceeded without the institution of private property rights and markets in land and in many cases was realized through migration to and clearing of new areas to farm cocoa and oil palm (in the forest belts) and cotton and groundnuts (in the savannah) — the four classic export crops of West Africa.

The second "macro-region" of labour reserves stretched from East through parts of Central to Southern Africa, in which there was widespread alienation of land to colonial settlers. The rationale of dispossessing Africans and concentrating them in "native reserves" was twofold: to provide land for white settlement and farms, and to enforce regular supplies of labour to these large farms and plantations, as well as to the mining complexes of the Rhodesias, Northern and Southern (now Zambia and Zimbabwe) and of South Africa, which drew in massive numbers of migrant miners from southern Mozambique, Nyasaland (now Malawi) and Basutoland (now Lesotho). Land alienation restricted African farmers to increasingly overcrowded and agriculturally marginal "native reserves" and subjected them to both economic and political pressures to secure their subsistence through periodic labour migration.

"Africa of the concessionary companies" is typified by the region of the Congo River basin, emblematic of an extremely brutal history of resource extraction and plunder to this day. The concessionary companies were granted vast territories for exploitation, with serious consequences for both their inhabitants and natural resources. Generally, however, they were unable to establish the conditions of more systematic and sustained capitalist agriculture, both settler and plantation, that came to prevail to the east (Kenya) and south (Southern Rhodesia/Zimbabwe and South Africa).

In most of sub-Saharan Africa, with the exception of the territories of most extensive European settlement, farmers, including pastoralists, were not dispossessed but "encouraged" to enter the monetary economy as producers of agricultural commodities and/ or labour power. The conditions of full proletarianization of the great majority of producers were not established, as Samir Amin and many others have emphasized. The means of "encouragement" — taxation and obligations to cultivate certain crops, provide labour service or enter migrant labour contracts — at first typically involved "forced commercialization," as in India, although colonial taxation in Africa was not based on land but on people in the form of hut and poll taxes and sometimes taxes on cattle as well. It is important to note, however, the initiative of some African farmers in pioneering commodity production for export by mobilizing land and labour through customary means, and without, or despite, the actions of colonial states. A famous example is cocoa production in Ghana from the early twentieth century, presented in the seminal study by Polly Hill (1963). The establishment and expansion of cocoa farming involved migration to initially sparsely populated forest areas and the recruitment of labour through particular forms of tenancy.

Substantial sections of African peasantries, then, prospered at particular times. This was especially the case when they were able to mobilize land and labour to integrate commodity production with their subsistence farming and to take advantage of buoyant international market conditions for their export crops, notably during the 1920s and in the two decades of the 1950s and 1960s, which spanned the end of the colonial period and the early days of independence. These success stories typically involved social differentiation in the countryside; some farmers benefitted more than others. At the same time, the vigour of peasant commodity production in different parts of Africa in the past contrasts painfully with the much more negative conditions of farming for most rural Africans today.

Patterns of Agrarian Change

The height of colonialism in Asia and Africa was reached during the consolidation of a capitalist world economy from the late nineteenth to the mid-twentieth century. In this period, the plantations of earlier periods of colonialism in the Caribbean, Latin America and Asia, were replaced by a new type of "industrial plantation." The frontiers of plantation production also expanded, especially in Southeast Asia and also in Central America and tropical zones of South America, by clearing large areas of tropical forest or encroaching on land cultivated by peasant farmers, as in Indonesia, the remaining principal colony of the Netherlands. Plantations required massive numbers of workers recruited from among poorer peasants and landless workers driven by economic necessity, often reinforced or directed by coercion. In short, the industrial plantation greatly enlarged the scale of its highly specialized monoculture, providing the world market with industrial crops like rubber, oil palm, cotton and sisal, and beverages and foods — tea, coffee, sugar, cocoa and bananas — that became items of mass consumption for the growing urban populations of industrialized countries.

Another pattern of pervasive change was the increased incorporation of the colonial peasantries of Asia and Africa as producers of export crops (cotton, oil palm, rubber, groundnuts, tobacco, coffee and cocoa), of food staples for domestic markets and export and of labour power, through labour migration to build railways and roads and to work in plantations, mines and ports. Processes of incorporation generated different types of class formation among the farming populations of the colonies (sometimes drawing on pre-existing social differences, like those of caste in India), now subject to the commodification of subsistence and with possibilities of accumulation for some.

Patterns of agrarian change in the later colonial period and following political independence have to be related to other dynamics and developments in the global economy, which I come back to in Chapters 4 and 5. To conclude here, I review three issues in debates about capitalism and colonialism. They connect with the questions at the end of Chapter 2 and also carry forward to the role of agrarian change in economic development in the South, following independence from colonial rule in Asia and Africa.[3]

Labour Regimes in Colonialism

I use the term "labour regime" to refer broadly to different methods of recruiting labour and their connections with how labour is organized in production (labour processes) and how it secures its subsistence. Four types of labour regimes have been indicated in this chapter: forced labour, semi-proletarianization, petty commodity production and proletarianization. We saw examples of forced labour regimes in the case of the Caribbean and Latin America, and forced labour also typified the earlier moments, at least, of subsequent colonialism in Asia and Africa. This was often tribute labour for construction of roads and railways, the arteries of colonial commerce, porterage and working in plantations and mines. Another type of forced labour regime was the indentured labour system, which, after the end of slavery in the British Empire, contracted millions of Indian and Chinese workers as wage workers for fixed periods, typically in plantations — in sugar in the Caribbean, South Africa, Mauritius and Fiji, and in rubber in Malaya (now Malaysia).

Table 3.2 summarizes key features of labour regimes under colonialism and helps to highlight certain analytical ideas. However,

Table 3.2 Labour Regimes in Colonialism

Labour regimes	Separation of producers from means of production	Extra-economic coercion	'Free' wage labour	Examples
1. Forced labour				
Slavery	complete	Yes	No	Caribbean, Brazil, southern U.S., 16c–19c
Tribute, tax in kind	No	Yes	No	Spanish America, 16c–17c; Africa, 19c–early 20c
Labour service	Partial	Yes	No	Spanish America, 16c on; Africa, Asia, 19c–early 20c
Indenture	Complete	Partial	"Transitional"	Caribbean, East Africa, Malaya, Mauritius, Fiji, 19c–20c
2. Semi-proletarian labour				
Wage labour + debt bondage	Partial or complete	No	"Transitional"	Spanish America, 17c on; Asia 19c–20c
Wage labour + own ("marginal") farming or other "self-employment"	Partial	No	"Transitional"	India and Africa, 19c; more generally 20c
3. "Family" labour ("peasant" petty commodity production)	No	No	No	India and Africa, 19c; more generally 20c
4. Proletarianization	Complete	No	Yes	Some sectors of colonial economies, starting 18c Latin America, 19c Asia, 20c Africa

it refers to only three "determinations" — the separation of producers from means of production, extra-economic coercion and "free" wage labour — of the many that always shape any concrete historical process (Marx, as quoted in the Introduction). For example, the use of "transitional" in several cells in the fourth column indicates that some types of wage labour regime do not require complete dispossession or "freedom" of their workers. This does not mean that "semi-proletarianized" workers necessarily occupy that "transitional" location only on a temporary or transitory basis. Indeed, some argue that, in many parts of the South, semi-proletarianization is a more common outcome of the commodification of subsistence than "full" proletarianization — another argument that similarly needs "concrete" specification of where, when and why that might be so (see further Chapter 7).

A second qualification relevant to Table 3.2 was noted in Chapter 2: that categories of rural labour, including distinctions between "free" and "unfree" labour, are often fluid and ambiguous in social reality. This is also expressed in the notion of "hybrid" forms of agrarian capitalism with "hybrid" labour regimes (Banaji 2010).

Finally, the table does not identify "family" labour enterprises in farming as tied by extra-economic coercion, even if a period of "forced commercialization" was needed initially to integrate them into commodity relations. Here I assume that by the end of the colonial period, household farmers were "locked into" commodity production by the "dull compulsion of economic forces" — the commodification of subsistence — just as proletarians and semi-proletarians are compelled to sell their labour power. I come back to this later too.

Recalling the two approaches outlined in Chapter 2, those who argue for the long histories of commercial capitalism consider forms of agrarian production established by European colonialism in Latin America, Asia and Africa as capitalist, however hybrid and fully or partly "unfree" their labour regimes. By contrast, those who argue for a strict (English-type) path of agrarian transition designate forms of agrarian production as "pre-capitalist' or otherwise "non-capitalist" if their labour regimes are not based on the employment by capital of properly "free" wage labour. At the same time, those forms of production might be regarded as contributing to primitive accumulation, which brings us to the second issue.

Was Colonialism Necessary for the Emergence of Capitalism?

For some scholars, capitalism began as a world system created through colonialism; hence they date its inception from the fateful moment of the arrival of Columbus in the New World in 1492. This provided the historical framework of Andre Gunder Frank's famous thesis of "the development of underdevelopment" in the Third World (Frank 1967) and, in a somewhat different version, informs the "modern world-system" of Immanuel Wallerstein (1979), in turn modified and developed by Arrighi and Moore (Chapter 2) among others.

This view might claim support from Marx, who wrote:

> The discovery of gold and silver in America, the extirpation, enslavement and entombment in mines of the aboriginal population, the beginnings of the conquest and looting of India, and the conversion of Africa into a preserve for the commercial hunting of black-skins, are all things which characterize the dawn of the era of capitalist production. (1976: 915)

Marx was echoed by the Bolshevik economist E. Preobrazhensky in the 1920s when he considered how "primitive socialist accumulation" might be achieved in the Soviet Union in the absence of the external sources of primitive accumulation that facilitated the emergence of capitalism: "the colonial policy of the world-trading countries... plundering in the form of taxes on the natives, seizure of their property, their cattle and land, their stores of precious metals, the conversion of conquered people into slaves, the infinitely varied system of crude cheating, and so on" (1965: 85).

Note that most of the *methods* of plunder in these passages from Marx and Preobrazhensky are also found in the historical records of expansion and conquest by pre-capitalist agrarian states and empires. For some scholars, this means that while direct and indirect colonialism might have facilitated the transition to capitalism in Europe, it could not provide *a sufficient condition* for it. That required the formation of a new social relation and structure of production, pioneered in the agrarian transition of England (and other parts of northwest Europe), which then led to industrial capitalism. This point can be used to help identify and contrast different phases and forms of European colonialism, from that of sixteenth-century Spain and Portugal — whether deemed "feudal" or "commercial" — to the capitalist colonialism of the British and French in the mid-nineteenth to mid-twentieth centuries. For example, the wealth and power of Spain in the sixteenth century, funded to a large degree by colonial silver, later gave way to relative economic backwardness as Britain and other parts of Europe underwent their transitions to agrarian and then industrial capitalism; in short, wealth is not the same as capital invested in developing production and productivity.[4] Is it also significant that a now backward Spain lost its American possessions in the first half of the nineteenth century, as industrial capitalism was fast developing elsewhere in Europe and a new type of colonialism was embarking on the most significant period of European rule in Asia and then Africa?

A debate continues to rage about whether primitive accumulation in the colonies made a significant contribution to economic growth in Europe, in particular from the late eighteenth century and especially as industrial capitalism moved into its "expansive" phase from the mid-nineteenth century. While much of the debate is about the causes of colonialism and its effects for capitalist development in Europe, those are distinct issues from its impact on colonial territories, including its sometimes massive, and often brutal, remakings of the organization of labour, land and farming. Perhaps the possibility that social and ecological upheaval, and even devastation, resulting from colonial conquest and exploitation, did *not* contribute significantly to accumulation in Europe, highlights even more the massive inequalities inscribed in the global development of capitalism.

The Economic Development of the Colonies?
Marx (1976: 91) suggested that countries in transition to capitalism can "suffer not only from the development of capitalist production, but also from the incompleteness of that development." Views of why capitalist development was "incomplete" in the colonies at the

time of their independence are often associated with the idea that the colonial incorporation of Latin America, Asia and Africa in an emergent capitalist world economy "underdeveloped" their societies. In terms of labour regimes, some argue that colonialism failed to transform the social relations of production, not least in farming, in a sufficiently capitalist manner. A provocative statement of this argument is that colonies were underdeveloped not because they were exploited but because they were "not exploited enough" (Kay 1975), that is, they were incompletely transformed in terms of capitalist production relations and their constant drive to increase the productivity of labour, hence the rate of exploitation (explained in Chapter 2). Incompleteness here refers to the persistence of pre- or non-capitalist relations in colonial economies, as an effect — intended or unintended — of colonial policies and the practices of colonial capital.

Another argument, which connects with the issue of primitive accumulation, is the "surplus drain" thesis: European powers organized colonial production and trade so as to extract its "surplus" (or profits) to their own benefit and that of their classes of capital — a kind of ongoing primitive accumulation that facilitated the development of industrial capitalism in Europe. Colonial economies were important sources of raw materials, both agricultural and mineral, produced by the "cheap labour" of peasants and semi-proletarianized workers. Industrialization was inhibited (as were more "advanced" forms of agrarian production in densely populated peasant areas) because the colonial powers wanted to prevent competition with their own industries and to keep colonies as "captive" markets for their exports of manufactured commodities. In this view, the incompleteness of capitalist development is registered in limited accumulation, hence formation of indigenous classes of capital, within colonial territories.

The colonial powers themselves — especially during the last phase of colonialism in the period of industrial capitalism — claimed that their mission was to bring civilization to the peoples of Asia and Africa, albeit in a suitably controlled and gradual fashion to avoid social and political disorder. This included economic development, understood as the extension of commodity relations, i.e., participation in markets and a monetary economy. The view that colonialism was "objectively necessary" to sow the seeds of capitalism in pre-capitalist societies of the South can also claim the support of Marx in the following way. Capitalism represents progress, however painful, because it is a more productive economic system than previous types of class society; it exploits labour more "efficiently" as the basis of a historically unprecedented, and continuous, development of the productive forces. Accordingly, with independence from colonial rule, the proper goal of strategies for economic growth, requiring active state intervention, was to extend and deepen the processes of capitalist development that colonialism had initiated. Failure to pursue that goal with adequate clarity and determination thus explains the relative lack of economic progress (Warren 1981; Sender and Smith 1986).

The issues highlighted in the last part of this chapter continue to resonate in debates about economic and social development in the South today. For example, do small-scale farmers in the South represent pre- or non-capitalist social relations and forms of production that hold back economic development? Do they represent an *anti*-capitalist type of farming and way of life that promise an alternative to the dominance of capitalist agriculture ("the peasant way" signalled in the Introduction)? If we discard notions of "persisting" and significant pre-capitalist elements in the economies of the South, does this simply shift the debate to ideas of more and less "advanced" forms of capitalism, which can be just as contentious (the third question at the end of Chapter 2)? And how are answers to all these and other questions affected by the uneven development of capitalism on a global scale (the fourth question at the end of Chapter 2)? The following chapters delve further into the issues these questions raise about the class dynamics of agrarian change since the end of colonialism.

Notes

1. Note that historians today often refer to the decades before 1914 as the first "golden age" of globalization.
2. In this respect, there are some parallels with the early colonial *hacienda* in Latin America (in the period of *encomienda*) and with feudal landed property more generally, and a contrast with the role of "improving

landlords" in the English and Japanese transitions outlined in Chapter 2.
3. To make things more complicated, different positions on these issues often claim support, more or less plausibly, from Marx's writings; moreover, Marx changed some of his ideas over time.
4. A similar point concerns why the great pre-capitalist agrarian civilizations did not develop industrial capitalism despite their wealth and power and, indeed, despite the fact that some were technologically more advanced than Europe at the beginning of the early modern period of world history — a point often made about China — and had their own significant elements of "commercial capitalism" (Pomeranz 2000; Goody 2004). During the period sketched in this chapter, all the political empires of those civilizations were overturned or otherwise collapsed: from the Aztecs and Incas in sixteenth-century Latin America to the Mughals of India in the eighteenth century and the Qing Dynasty of China in the nineteenth, and the final demise, as a result of the First World War, of the remaining old empires of Eurasia: those of the Hapsburgs (Austro-Hungary), the Romanovs (Russia) and the Ottomans (Turkey and its possessions).

Chapter 4

Farming and Agriculture, Local and Global

Chapters 2 and 3 highlighted general themes — changes in the uses of land and labour, and in class dynamics — in the making of the modern world, from the origins and early development of capitalism to the end of the colonial period. In doing so, they indicated several expansions of scale, for example, in the size of farming enterprises in different places at different times, in the geographical reach of trade in agricultural commodities and in the volume and value of trade.

This chapter takes a different but complementary perspective. It considers issues of increasing scale with special reference to two connected processes. One is how farming, once the most localized of activities, becomes part of "agriculture" or the "agricultural sector." The other is how geographical expansions of agricultural markets in capitalism, and their sources of demand and supply, rest on an increase in social scale through the extension and "deepening" of commodity relations and their social divisions of labour.

The terms "farming" and "agriculture" are commonly used interchangeably, which I have avoided, apart from describing what is produced on farms — crops and animals — as "agricultural." Rather I rely on the term "agrarian" to describe the social relations and practices of farming, societies based on farming and processes of change in farming. It is useful to distinguish between farming and agriculture as we consider agrarian change, especially since the 1870s. The significance of this period was indicated in chapter 3 and is explored further here until the 1970s to illustrate the following key aspects of shifts from farming to agriculture:

- the industrial basis of technical change;
- the formation of global markets and divisions of labour in agri-

culture, and especially staple foods; and
- the constitution of the "agricultural sector" as an object of policy.

As in chapters 2 and 3, here I provide only broad historical outlines and selective examples that contextualize particular ideas and issues. Chapter 5 brings the story up to date.

From Farming to Agriculture

In his excellent book on the formation of a global economy, Herman Schwartz notes:

> [Before industrial capitalism] hardly anyone ever transported grain overland for more than 20 miles [hence] virtually all economic, social and political life took place in microeconomies centered on market towns surrounded by an agricultural hinterland of about 20 miles.... From the fifteenth century to the end of the nineteenth century, agriculture lay at the heart of the global economy (and naturally most "local" economies as well)... Food and agriculturally derived raw materials accounted for over half of international trade as late as 1929. (2000: 13)

While these two observations seem to be in tension with each other, they are useful for thinking about the shifts from farming to agriculture that I suggest here. Following from the first observation, farming is what farmers do and have done through millennia: cultivate the soil and raise livestock, or some combination of the two, typically within a system of established fields and demarcated pastures. Farmers have always had to manage the natural conditions of their activity, with all their uncertainties and risks, including the vagaries of climate (rainfall and temperature) and the biochemical tendency to soil degradation unless measures are taken to maintain or restore the fertility of land. Successful farming, then, requires high levels of knowledge of ecological conditions and a willingness to devise and adopt better methods of cultivation within acceptable boundaries of uncertainty and risk. Even (or especially) farmers using so-called simple technologies — hand tools like digging sticks, hoes, machetes and axes — demonstrate considerable capacities of small-scale experimentation and accumulation of knowledge, as anthropologist Paul Richards' detailed study of rice farmers in Sierra Leone (1986) showed.

Recalling some of the elements described in chapter 1, the minimum *social* conditions of farming include access to land, labour, tools and seeds. Historically, the principal social unit through which the means of farming were secured and farming conducted is the rural household. Once more (as with the terms "property" and "income", noted earlier) this observation needs a warning: farming households in different societies at different times vary greatly in their size, composition and social relations within the household (notably gender relations) and with other households in rural communities.

Before industrial capitalism, farming was limited in both its social and spatial scales. It was embedded in relatively simple social divisions of labour, and non-farming groups or classes generally had little impact on how farmers farmed. There are qualifications of this simple picture, of course. Sometimes outside institutions provided important conditions of production that individual farming households or villages could not provide for themselves. The best-known example is the construction and maintenance by the state of major irrigation works in East Asia (Bray 1986), as well as in Western Asia (Mesopotamia), North Africa (Egypt) and pre-colonial Central America (Mexico). Another important qualification relates to entrepreneurial landowners in the vanguard of commercial capitalism (chapter 2) who actively managed labour processes on their estates. A third is provided by the fascinating histories of the diffusion of food staples, other crops and livestock from their places of origin to other regions where they were adopted, sometimes with profound ecological and social consequences (Grigg 1974: Ch 3; Crosby 1986, on the "ecological imperialism" of settler colonialism in the Americas and elsewhere). A fourth example is where *waterborne* transport makes it relatively easy to carry and trade agricultural products in bulk. Agrarian civilizations, especially in arid regions, typically originated in great river basins, sources of irrigation that also facilitated the transport by barge and boat of grain to feed courts, armies and non-farming populations in towns and cities (typically established on rivers). Maritime transport was key to the agricultural trade of the Mediterranean, for example, from ancient times.

However, for most of its history until relatively recently farming was an extremely *localized* activity and way of life.[1] The localism of farming includes the following:

- maintaining soil fertility through the use of "green" and animal manures sourced on or near the farm, as well as through systems of fallow and crop rotation — termed "closed-loop agro-ecological systems";
- the pooling of labour between neighbouring households at critical moments of the farming calendar, for example, to ensure timely planting and harvesting, especially when weather conditions are uncertain; and
- the provision by local artisans of goods and services farmers might not produce themselves, including some of the tools they used.

The combination of farming with household handicraft production like spinning and weaving, to take a common example, was widespread and was destroyed over time by the development of capitalism and its drive towards specialization in the social division of labour. Marx observed this for England, and Bagchi suggested it for India (chapter 3 above), where the impact of colonialism was to *increase* "ruralization" and "peasantization," that is, an economically more narrow existence in the countryside.

In agrarian societies before the advent of capitalism — in both its European heartlands and colonial conditions — farming was what most people did. What we call "agriculture" was then simply an aggregation, the sum total, of farmers and their activities. Farmers connected with non-farmers to some degree through the exactions of rents and taxes and through typically localized exchange but were not affected by the wider divisions of labour, processes of technological change and market dynamics that came to characterize the "agricultural sector" in industrial capitalism.

The notion of the "agricultural sector" was invented and applied in the emergence and development of "modern," that is, capitalist, economies. Marx noted that social divisions of labour between agriculture and industry, and between countryside and town, emerged as characteristic features of the development of capitalism. It only made sense to distinguish an agricultural sector when an industrial sector was rising to prominence in the North and, subsequently, when industrialization became the main economic objective of "national development" in the countries of the South following their independence from colonial rule.

By "agriculture" or the "agricultural sector" in modern capitalist economies, I mean farming *together with* all those economic interests and their specialized institutions and activities, "upstream" and "downstream" of farming, that affect the activities and reproduction of farmers. "Upstream" refers to the conditions of production necessary to undertake farming and how those conditions are secured. This includes the supply of instruments of labour, or "inputs" (tools, fertilizers, seeds), as well as markets for land, labour and credit — and crucially, of course, the mobilization of labour. "Downstream" refers to what happens to crops and animals when they leave the farm — their marketing, processing and distribution — and how those activities affect farmers' incomes, which are necessary to reproducing themselves. Powerful agents upstream and downstream of farming in capitalist agriculture today are exemplified by agri-input capital and agro-food capital respectively, terms used by Weis (2007).

In capitalism, agriculture becomes increasingly defined as a distinct sector in terms of its place in social divisions of labour and as an object of public policy. Both link to each other and to that central dynamic emphasized earlier: the commodification of subsistence, through which once largely self-sufficient farmers come to rely increasingly on markets (commodity exchange) for their reproduction. In effect, they come to depend on a money income: to pay taxes and/or rent in cash (rather than in kind or in labour service); to buy consumption goods they can no longer supply from their own labour or source from the local economy; and to buy their means of production — fertilizers, seeds, tools and other farm equipment.[2]

The period from the 1870s to today is one of revolutionary change in the technical conditions of farming, in contrast to the evolutionary change that characterized its long history before then, which involved cautious and gradual innovation in the breeding of improved plants and animals and in improved methods of cultivation and land husbandry. Even the earlier transitions to capitalist farming in England from the sixteenth-century onward did not generate a technical revolution comparable with what happened later.[3]

The historical dividing line of the 1870s marks the impact of the second industrial revolution, mentioned in chapter 3. While the material basis of the first industrial revolution was iron, coal and steam power, that of the second was steel, chemicals, electricity and petroleum. Over time — and accelerating from the 1940s — the second industrial revolution and its innovations transformed the following three aspects of productivity in farming (introduced in chapter 1):

- the impact of chemical fertilizers and other agricultural chemicals on the productivity of land (yields);
- similarly the impact of scientific plant and animal breeding (facilitated by new knowledge of genetics and its applications) on yields; and
- the internal combustion engine and its use in tractors and other farm machines transformed the productivity of labour.

"Nature's Metropolis" and the First International Food Regime (1870s–1914)

Recalling Schwartz's observation (above), for most of the five centuries of the global economy he refers to, transport of agricultural commodities in bulk relied mainly on water: rivers, lakes, seas and oceans. The first agricultural commodity regularly transported in bulk across oceanic distances was sugar from the slave plantations of Brazil and the Caribbean. The revolution in overland transport that greatly extended the scale of international trade in agricultural commodities was the invention and spread of the railway: the equivalent of oceanic transport in its ability to cross great distances. Rail meant that the prairies of Argentina, Australia, Canada and above all the U.S. could become the world's major exporters of grain and meat. This was the basis of the first international food regime (IFR), from 1870 to 1914:

the "first price-governed [international] market in an essential means of life" (Friedmann 2004: 125). It was a "settler-colonial" regime, in Friedmann's term, that "opened" vast frontiers of mostly virgin land, sparsely populated and little cultivated previously, to extensive wheat farming and cattle ranching for export to Europe, which was rapidly urbanizing and increasingly dependent on imports of staple foods.

The key site, then, in terms of the subsequent history of capitalist agriculture, was not northwestern Europe, where the first transitions to capitalist farming occurred. Rather it was exemplified by the vast prairies of the U.S. Midwest, which generated the growth of Chicago: *Nature's Metropolis* as William Cronon (1991) described it. In the second half of the nineteenth century, Chicago and its farming hinterland, increasingly enlarged by the development of the railway, pioneered the close interlinkages of the following aspects of agriculture:

- extensive grain monoculture (to feed both people and livestock);
- the slaughter of cattle and processing of meat by industrial means and on a truly industrial scale;
- the industrial manufacture of farm equipment (notably the steel plough and later tractors);
- infrastructure for handling and transporting grain and meat (which required refrigeration) in unprecedented quantities over long distances; and
- futures markets and other institutional innovations in financing the production and trade of agricultural commodities.

In effect, Chicago pioneered many aspects of modern agribusiness, which came to incorporate and shape farming. It also exemplified the "temperate grain-livestock complex," which was central to international agricultural trade and divisions of labour from the 1870s onwards.

European farmers, who were unable to compete with cheaper imported grain, responded by turning to more intensive production of higher value products, like dairy, fruit and vegetables, and by abandoning farming and leaving the countryside. Outside these two principal zones of temperate farming, and complementing them, was the tropical agricultural production and exports of Asia and Africa, whose colonial incorporation was completed in the same period. The "industrial plantation" of this period (chapter 3) provides a tropical and colonial counterpart to the shift from farming to agriculture exemplified by the U.S. Midwest. What distinguished the industrial plantation from earlier forms of plantation were the connections between its organization and methods of production, its ownership structures and its close linkages with finance capital, shipping, industrial processing and manufacturing — aspects of a "worldwide shift towards agribusiness" in the late nineteenth century, remarked by Ann Stoler (1985: 17) in her study of plantations in Sumatra. Like the prairies of the temperate grain-livestock complex, many zones of industrial plantation production were also new agricultural frontiers, in this case established by clearing vast areas of tropical forest.

In short, a global division of labour in agricultural production and trade emerged from the 1870s, comprising the following:

- new zones of grain and meat production in the "neo-Europes" (Crosby 1986), established by settler colonialism in the temperate Americas, Southern Africa, Australia and New Zealand;
- more diversified patterns of farming in parts of Europe itself at the same time as accelerating rural out-migration; and
- specialization in tropical export crops in colonial Asia and Africa and the tropical zones of the former colonies of Central and South America, whether grown on peasant or capitalist farms, or on industrial plantations.

A central element of this global division of labour and its economic dynamic was a shift from farming to agriculture, which connected revolutionary changes in the technical conditions and organization of production (especially in the "neo-Europes" and Europe itself and in the industrial plantations of the tropics) with the vastly expanded scale of international trade in the staple foods of the temperate grain-livestock complex, in "tropical groceries" — foods and beverages like sugar, cocoa, bananas, tea, coffee — and in mostly tropical industrial crops like rubber, palm oil, cotton, sisal and jute.

4 / FARMING AND AGRICULTURE, LOCAL AND GLOBAL

With regard to agriculture as an object of policy, on the supply side of the first IFR,

> Settler agriculture cheapened agricultural commodity production, via the political appropriation and colonization of new lands.... Specialized commodity production... [was] actively promoted by settler states via land and immigration policy, and the establishment of social infrastructure, mainly railways and credit facilities. (Friedmann and McMichael 1989: 101)

On the demand side, the way to a relatively free trade order was prepared by the 1846 repeal of the Corn Laws in Britain, which had protected British farmers and landowners, and their commercial rents, from cheaper imported grain.[4] While repeal occurred before the historical watershed of the 1870s, it connects with it in several ways. In the 1840s, Britain had the first class of industrial capital confident in its international competitive strength and ability to take on the domestic "agricultural interest" in the interests of "free trade," including cheaper imported food to keep wages, hence labour costs, low. The repeal of the Corn Laws and the subsequent enforcement by Britain of similar measures on other European countries paved the way for the relatively free trade order of the "international food regime" that emerged several decades later, when British grain farming experienced serious competitive pressures as wheat imports started to arrive in rapidly growing quantities.[5]

Chapter 3 sketched some of the characteristic policies of colonial states in Asia and Africa in this period that imposed the commodification of subsistence on peasant farmers and facilitated the creation of industrial plantations, settler farming and commercial forestry. The commodification of subsistence could take, and combine, different forms of activity in expanding and deepening social divisions of labour: including pressures on peasant farmers to cultivate specialized export crops, to produce food for a growing wage labour force in mining, construction, maunfacturing and industrial plantations and to engage in seasonal wage labour. From the nineteenth-century too, colonial governments established Departments of Agriculture in their Asian and African territories, with agricultural research in the colonial period concentrated on major export crops like rubber and sugar, largely neglecting the food staples of the tropics.

Finally, as noted in chapter 3, there were also agricultural frontiers created by indigenous farmers, who migrated and cleared land to cultivate new export crops. While they did so on their own initiative, during this period and subsequently, specialized export production increasingly integrated them with capitalist companies that traded, shipped and processed their crops. One aspect of integration was the development of quality standards and regulation in the international trade of such tropical products as coffee, cocoa and rubber (Daviron 2002).

From Free Trade to Protectionism (1914–1940s)

The capitalist world economy was profoundly affected by the world wars of 1914–1918 and 1939–1945 and the great depression of the 1930s, with its consequences for international trade. Subject to the usual unevenness of capitalist development in different parts of the world and despite the shrinking of the world economy, the processes described above continued with one crucial exception. The first IFR collapsed in 1914, and wartime policies, together with the depression, generated widespread protectionism of agriculture in the industrial capitalist countries.[6] One example, which was key to what happened later, was the introduction of a comprehensive farm support policy in the U.S. in the 1930s as part of the "New Deal" of the Roosevelt governments.[7] This policy guaranteed minimum, or "floor," prices to farmers, with surplus stocks — grain that could not be sold at prevailing market prices — held by the government.

At the same time, Britain, France and other European colonial powers tried to squeeze even more out of the subject farming populations of Asia and Africa. The marketing boards for key agricultural commodities that emerged to support farmers (and agricultural industries more broadly) in Europe were adapted in colonial Africa to extract larger revenues from its farmers. In India, the great depression intensified the existing pattern of displacing staple food cultivation for domestic consumption with export production of cotton, jute, sugar and fine grains, thereby contributing to the great Bengal famine of 1943–44 (chapter 3).

The Second International Food Regime (1940s–1970s)

Key features of the post-Second World War period were the emergence of the U.S. and U.S.S.R. as rival "super powers"; their competition for allies among the countries of Asia and Africa as they achieved independence (which both super powers supported, for different reasons); and the recovery and extraordinary expansion of the capitalist world economy from the 1950s to the early 1970s. These features helped shape the development of agriculture, and its effects for farming, in the three main regions of the global division of labour, outlined above.

In the U.S. and the industrialized North generally, from the late 1940s there was a marked acceleration in the rate of technical transformation of farming through "chemicalization" (fertilizers, pesticides, herbicides), mechanization and the development of high-yielding seeds and animals (bred for ever higher yields of milk and meat). The accelerated technical transformation of Northern farming, in significant part, expressed the growing size and concentration of agri-input corporations upstream of farming. Their role in shaping farming methods also contributed to tendencies to concentration in farming, with fewer, larger and more capitalized farms, hence increasing scale and growing labour productivity. From 1950 to 1972, those working in farming in the U.S. declined from 15 to 5 percent of the total labour force (Friedmann 1990: 24). Other effects included the rapid growth of the gap in labour and land productivity between large-scale capitalist farmers in both North and South and small-scale farmers concentrated in the South, as noted in chapter 1.

This soon generated the familiar problem of capitalism, analyzed by Marx, of overproduction: when capitalist competition and productivity growth generate quantities of commodities that cannot be sold because of lack of "effective demand" — an economists' term for whether there is enough purchasing power to buy the commodities on offer. In turn, this reflects a fundamental feature of capitalism: that "effective demand" expresses who gets what — the "disposable incomes" consumers are able to spend (including on credit) — and not who *needs* what. This is an especially pointed theme in debates about today's global food economy, in which there is no absolute shortage of food production, but many people, lacking enough income to buy adequate food, go hungry.

In the U.S., continuing government policies of "farm support" — in fact, agricultural industry support — contributed to this problem but also found a "solution," at least for a while, in the formation of a second international food regime. This centred on the disposal of U.S. food surpluses as food aid, first to assist the post-war reconstruction of Western Europe and then to the Third World, where food aid was a strategic part of foreign policy during the Cold War. Friedmann (2004) calls this "the mercantile-industrial food regime": mercantile because it subsidized production and managed trade to the benefit of U.S., and also European, agricultural interests, including giant grain trading companies, while also serving foreign policy interests in the Third World; and industrial because of the growing importance within it of agri-input corporations.

Unlike the largely price-governed first international food regime, with its competitive pressures on European grain farming, the second IFR combined "mercantile" trade policies with "the corporate organization of a transnational agro-food complex centred on the Atlantic economy" (Friedmann 1993: 18). In this complex, European countries replicated the "national" character of U.S. agricultural policy in supporting farm production and exports under the Common Agricultural Policy (CAP) of what is now the European Union.[8]

Rising real incomes in the North during the post-war economic boom were reflected in increased consumption and indeed a new mass culture of consumerism. In particular, the everyday consumption of meat and processed and convenience foods increased greatly, which signalled the enhanced prominence of the agro-food industries downstream of farming in the "transnational agro-food complex."

Engel's Law, formulated by German statistician Ernst Engel (1821–1896), states that as income rises the proportion spent on food decreases. In the technical terms of economics, the "income elasticity of demand for food" is less than 1, which means that of each additional unit of disposable income, only part — and a diminishing part — is spent on food. However, this does not mean that less money is spent on food. To take a simple example, say a household with an annual income of $10,000 spends 10 percent of that, $1,000, on food. Over time its income doubles to $20,000 and the proportion it spends on food drops to 7 percent, or $1,400, an increase of 40 percent in the *amount* it spends on food.[9] In short, the agro-food industries expanded and compete to supply — and to stimulate — the total amount spent on food. From the 1950s especially, and on an ever larger economic and geographical scale today (chapter 5), some of the biggest names in the agro-food industries took off, not least those in sourcing and slaughtering livestock and processing meat and those in the now globalized fast food chains.

For the South, wheat imports from the U.S. and later the E.U., initially under the concessional terms of food aid, could provide food more cheaply than domestic farming to boost industrialization in countries that had been largely self-sufficient in food production (echoing the case of Britain after the repeal of the Corn Laws a century or so earlier). This is emphasized in Friedmann's account of the "origins of Third World food dependence" (1990), exemplified by parts of Latin America, North Africa and Western Asia.

Agricultural Modernization in the Moment of Developmentalism (1950s–1970s)

The newly independent countries of Asia and Africa emerged from colonialism still largely agrarian societies but now committed to "national development," as were most Latin American countries, which were generally more industrialized.[10] Modernizing agriculture was usually a central element of ideas about "national development," if often subordinated to the desire for industrialization. Giving priority to industrialization could mean substituting domestic grain production with cheap wheat imports or "postponing" agricultural modernization until the development of national industry could provide it with modern inputs. The latter was the dominant view of development planning in India for the first twenty years of independence, before the Green Revolution was launched.

During the peak period of "developmentalism" — the pursuit

of state-led development — from the 1950s to 1970s, a wide range of policy measures was adopted and applied by governments in the South to "modernize" their agriculture. Agricultural policy was also used to try to resolve some of the contradictions and social tensions inherited from their colonial histories, no less in Latin America than in Asia and Africa. Thus, for example, land reforms, of very different kinds, were widespread in this period (see chapter 6), as was government-sponsored or imposed resettlement of rural populations (a familiar colonial practice), for example, in parts of Africa and Southeast Asia. The "integrated rural development programs" (IDRPs) of the 1970s, a comprehensive "package" including delivery of education and health as well as economic services to the countryside, were promoted especially strongly by the World Bank and the U.S. Agency for International Development (USAID), which some interpreted as their response to the success of a peasant-based and communist-led war of national liberation in Vietnam.

In this period, agricultural and rural development policies exhibited a lot of institutional variety and frequent "paradigm shifts," or more simply, changing fashions, as they do today.[11] Despite their variety, policies and programs of modernization shared a core logic: promoting a *more productive agriculture based in deepening commodity relations*, whether through "smallholder" development or larger-scale farming, public and private. This was often pursued by governments in the South in "partnership" with the World Bank, bilateral aid donors, notably the U.S., Britain and France, and private agribusiness capital (national and international), all of which supplied designs for modernization.

"*More productive*" addresses the technical conditions of farming: improved varieties and cultivation methods, greater fertilizer use and "soft" credit and technical advice to farmers (promoted through extension services). This was typically done on a crop basis, for both export and food crops, most famously during the Green Revolution from the 1960s with its high yielding variety (HYV) seeds of the "big three" grains of maize, wheat and rice.[12] The "package" combined HYV seeds with fertilizers, requiring substantial irrigation to produce larger harvests, as illustrated in the vignette from northern India in the Introduction.

"*Deepening commodity relations*" involves greater integration of farmers in markets, in which they specialize in producing particular commodities for sale, as well as buying and using greater quantities of means of production ("modern" inputs) and means of consumption, which might include food. The means to this end commonly included the following:

- credit schemes for seasonal production expenses and fixed capital investments, through state agricultural banks or other public bodies;
- subsidies on fertilizers and, in irrigated areas of India, on electricity to power tube wells and pumps;
- facilitating marketing by upgrading transport infrastructure and specialized organizations like cooperatives and para-statal agricultural agencies (some adapted from the colonial period, like crop marketing boards);
- "administered" prices, especially minimum or "floor" prices, set by governments for key crops.

I was living in Tanzania in the 1970s, when the para-statal crop agencies expanded greatly to encompass research and development, input and credit supply, transport, storage and processing as well as marketing. This struck me as an attempt to emulate, in very different conditions, the ways in which corporations upstream and downstream of farming in the North integrated and controlled the "agricultural sector" (Bernstein 1981). Jonathan Barker (1989) described such programs of agricultural modernization in sub-Saharan Africa as an attempt to create "state peasantries."

It is difficult to generalize about the effects of agricultural modernization efforts during the moment of "developmentalism" because of the variety of policy measures, of their technical and institutional "packages" and of government capacities in delivering them and because of the even greater variety of ecological conditions and types of farming to which they were applied. In fact, assessing the impact of policies — a sizeable profession in itself — is always challenging because agricultural "performance" is affected by many other factors, from weather to the effects of macroeconomic policies (for example, and notably, concerning exchange rates of currencies and interest rates), to the vagaries of markets and prices, locally and internationally. There were some success stories on different scales, of which the largest was the Green Revolution in India, which enabled it to become self-sufficient in grain production in a short time. This is not to say that the "success" of the Green Revolution was unqualified; there are limits to the growth of wheat and rice yields derived from its biochemical "packages" and issues of its environmental costs, hence sustainability, in some areas. Not all farmers benefitted equally from the implementation of the Green Revolution (see chapter 7), nor food consumers from its effects. For example, some of the land devoted to growing the higher quality and more expensive grains was diverted from "coarse" grains, like millet, and from pulses, a key source of protein in the diets of the poor.

Conclusion

Answering the question of which farmers benefit from different agricultural policies, and from processes of agrarian change in capitalism more broadly, involves examining their differentiation, a major theme in Chapters 7 and 8. Before considering the current period of neo-liberal globalization in the next chapter, I conclude here with an observation on the prospect of achieving economic development today, including industrialization, through agricultural export-led growth, compared with earlier periods of the formation of the global capitalist economy.

Earlier transitions to industrial capitalism, and the contributions to them of agriculture, occurred when prices for agricultural commodities were generally much higher in real terms than they are now. The international terms of trade "moved in favour of agriculture... through the nineteenth century and indeed up to the First World War," whereas since the 1940s they mostly "turned sharply against agricultural commodities and in favour of manufactured goods for the first time since the industrial revolution" (Kitching 2001: 154–5). In part this reflects the massive growth in the productivity of farming in the North. For much of the South, the promotion of exports of tropical agricultural commodities, in the moment of developmentalism and beyond (chapter 5), tends to generate systematic overproduction, which depresses their prices in international markets (coffee being perhaps the best-known example).

Gavin Kitching (2001) also reminds us that today's richest countries had smaller populations and rates of population growth at the time of their industrial take-off than the principal countries of the South today. Industrial technologies were generally more labour-intensive too than they are now; hence industry needed and was better able to absorb the labour of migrants from rural areas displaced by primitive accumulation and the development of capitalist farming. Even so, we can note that during the first "golden age" of globalization, the exodus of small farmers and agricultural workers from European countrysides contributed, in very large numbers, to transatlantic migration to North and South America.

Notes

1. Local should not be confused with "static". The long histories of farming involved movement to clear and settle new areas for cultivation — in effect, to create new localities.
2. Note, however, that some theorists argue that the formation of capitalist agriculture does not mean that the *farming* it incorporates is necessarily capitalist. I come back to this in chapters 6 and 7.
3. Some historians argue that the significant gains in yields from capitalist "high farming" in England from the sixteenth to eighteenth centuries rested on labour-intensive methods, without any marked increase in the productivity of labour.
4. Note that "corn" here was wheat, not "corn" in the American sense of maize.
5. Note too the continuing importance of this issue to agricultural politics and development policies today: the price of food relative to that of industrial goods, or the "terms of trade" between the agricultural and industrial sectors within countries *and* in international trade; see further below.
6. The collapse of the IFR, and emergence of protectionism, is sometimes dated as 1929, the onset of the great depression.
7. The New Deal was a program of public investment, among other things, to combat massive unemployment in order to revive economic growth.
8. The CAP was initiated in 1962 and today accounts for nearly half of

E.U. budget expenditure.
9. In contrast, poor households in the South have to to spend a very large proportion of their much smaller incomes on food, and even then can not afford adequate diets; there is a glimpse of this in the vignette of the Bangladeshi sharecropper in the Introducion.
10. In some cases, like Brazil and Chile, they had experienced significant industrial growth when world trade declined during the 1930s, through "import substitution": producing manufactured goods that they had previously imported.
11. This is a common syndrome. Conventional development models aim for "win-win" scenarios — to achieve both economic growth and an end to poverty — but their prescriptions are confounded by the inequalities and contradictions of capitalism; hence the need to invent apparently "new" ideas and approaches, or reinvent and re-label old ones, which then confront the same problems in practice.
12. In fact, the Green Revolution started with the development of HYVs in the U.S. in the 1930s, a story told in an important study by Jack Kloppenburg (2004).

Chapter 5

Neoliberal Globalization and World Agriculture

Beginning in the 1970s, the capitalist world economy has undergone a process of profound change, commonly termed globalization. The significance and meaning of contemporary globalization, the reasons for it and its effects remain highly controversial. At its broadest, it refers to new forms of the restructuring of capital on a world scale and includes the following features:

- deregulation of financial markets and "financialization" of all aspects of economic activity;
- increasing deregulation of international trade;
- shifts in the production, sourcing and sales strategies and technologies of transnational agribusiness and manufacturing corporations; and
- massive possibilities attendant on information technologies, not least for organizing economic activity (production and marketing) and for mass communications.

In retrospect, the 1970s seems to have been as definitive a marker of subsequent structural shifts in the world economy as was the 1870s, a century before. Today's globalization was similarly triggered by recession in the world capitalist economy and its "adjustments," which led to a massive expansion of international flows of commodities and above all of money. It is also marked by the declining competitiveness of U.S. industry (as previously of British industry). Beverly Silver and Giovanni Arrighi (2000: 56) put it like this: "The deep capitalist crisis of the 1970s was first and foremost a reflection of the inability of world capitalism as instituted under US hegemony to deliver on the promises of a Global New Deal"[1] — which included support of "developmentalism" in the South, if selectively so. This led to "a liquidation of the labour-friendly and development-friendly international regime of the preceding thirty years in favour of a capital-friendly regime." "Friendly" here is relative to what went before and what came next: "Under the new regime, the crisis of capitalism quickly turned into a crisis of organised labour and of the welfare state in rich countries, and of the crisis of Communism and of the developmental state in poorer countries."

The term *"neoliberal* globalization" suggests that the changes and dynamics of the current period are not simply the "automatic" effects of the cyclical nature and contradictions of capitalism (e.g., overproduction, over-accumulation and its pressures on the rate of profit) but represent a particular ideological and political program — neoliberalism — to resolve the problems of capital (Harvey 2005, especially chapter 2), a program that replaced the previous political attempts to construct a "Global New Deal," as Silver and Arrighi call it. The neoliberal program centres on promoting the freedom and mobility of capital and on "rolling back the state," albeit highly selectively in practice.

First, this means reducing or abolishing the gains of working classes, registered in state regulation and provision concerning employment contracts, working hours and conditions, minimum wages, rights of association, health care, education and social insurance and pensions. Second, global capital markets — unrestricted by regulation and in which vast amounts of money move with unprecedented speed, driven by the pursuit of short-term gains — undermine the capacities of states to pursue national macroeconomic policies with any effective autonomy.Thus, the neoliberal mantra of policy to achieve "competitiveness" in global markets and the agenda of privatizing public enterprises and services are aspects of a deepening commodification of all aspects of social existence. Third, in terms of economic development, neoliberalism includes the structural adjustment programs, economic liberalization, privatizations and "state reform" agenda imposed on the countries of the South (and former Soviet bloc) that spelled the end of the project of state-led development.

5 / NEOLIBERAL GLOBALIZATION AND WORLD AGRICULTURE

Collapse of the Second International Food Regime

The collapse of the second IFR parallels the timing and dynamics of globalization more broadly. The collapse began in the early 1970s, triggered by "a sudden, unprecedented shortage and sky-rocketing prices" in world grain markets, as the U.S. lifted its embargo on grain sales to the Soviet Union and supplied it with enormous quantities of wheat at preferential prices (Friedmann 1993: 40). This episode registered the contradiction of overproduction, hence surplus disposal and the escalating costs of maintaining price stability, with effects for the "mercantile" side of the second IFR. Europe also contributed to overproduction as it had replicated U.S. policies of agricultural support and started to produce peacetime grain surpluses for the first time in a century (as well as large surpluses of other commodities like dairy products).

Intensified competition in international agricultural trade linked the strains of managing the "mercantile" side of the second IFR with the changing geography of its "industrial" (production) side. For example, Argentina and Brazil became two of the world's four biggest producers of soy (the others being the U.S. and China). Soy, an oilseed, is mostly converted to an animal feed for intensive livestock production in feedlots. Its production has continued to expand massively, doubling from 1990 to 2005, and it has joined the "big three" grains of wheat, rice and maize to make up the "big four" of world field crops (Weis 2007: 17). The story of soy illustrates the accelerated growth in power, influence and control of global food sourcing, processing and sales by transnational agribusiness, both agri-input and agro-food, which now pushed against the "mercantile" limits of the second IFR, from which it had benefitted earlier. Corporations became "the major (global) agents attempting to... organize stable conditions of production and consumption which allow them to plan investment, sourcing of agricultural materials, and marketing" (Friedmann 1993: 52). In effect, this marks a shift towards *private* (corporate) regulation of the global food economy, albeit with continuing high levels of agricultural subsidies in the U.S. and the E.U.

In terms of the politics of agricultural interests, the end of the Cold War and demise of the U.S.S.R. undermined the strategic purpose of the transatlantic pivot of the second IFR (including food aid), while recurrent problems of overproduction led the U.S. to put agricultural trade on the agenda of the GATT (General Agreement on Tariffs and Trade) in the Uruguay round of 1986–1994, having previously blocked its subjection to GATT processes and rules.[2]

Global Agriculture in the Moment of Neoliberalism

From the agricultural world market disorder that followed the collapse of the second IFR, a third IFR may be taking shape: an emergent "multilateral trade-corporate food regime" (Friedmann 2004). "Multilateral trade," the international competition just noted, replaces the "mercantile" aspect of the second IFR, while its "industrial" aspect continues, now under increasing corporate control both upstream and downstream of farming. Whether a third IFR, accompanied by attempts to regulate and resist it, can achieve the same degree of coherence and relative stability as the previous two is an open question, not least in the face of such environmental pressures as the depletion of oil reserves and climate change. It is striking that the dramatic global inflation in grain prices that began in 2005, and peaked in 2008, replicated (if not for identical reasons) that of the 1970s, the beginning of the end of the second IFR.

The following key themes characterize the discussion of neoliberal globalization and its impact on agriculture over recent decades:

1. trade liberalization, shifts in the global trade patterns of agricultural commodities and associated battles within and around the WTO;
2. the effects on world market prices of futures trading in agricultural commodities, that is, speculation spurred by "financialization";
3. the removal of subsidies and other forms of support to small farmers in the South as "austerity" measures required by neoliberalism, together with reduction of government and aid budgets for most farming in the South;
4. the increasing concentration of global corporations in both agri-input and agro-food industries, marked by mergers and

acquisitions and the economic power of fewer corporations commanding larger market shares;
5. new organizational technologies deployed by these corporations along commodity chains from farming through processing and manufacturing to retail distribution, e.g., the "supermarket revolution" in the global sourcing of food and market shares of food sales and the recent entry of major supermarket chains into China, India and other parts of the South;
6. the combination of these organizational technologies with corporate economic power, which shapes and constrains the practices and "choices" of farmers and consumers;
7. the push by corporations to patent intellectual property rights in genetic plant material, under the provisions of the WTO on Trade-Related Aspects of Intellectual Property Rights (TRIPS), and the issue of corporate "biopiracy";
8. the technical frontier of engineering plant and animal genetic material (GMOs, or genetically modified organisms) that, together with specialized monoculture, contributes to the loss of biodiversity;
9. the profit frontier of biofuel production, dominated by agribusiness corporations supported by public subsidies in the U.S. and Europe, and its effects for world grain production for human consumption;
10. the health consequences, including rising levels of toxic chemicals in "industrially" grown and processed foods, nutritional deficiencies of diets composed of junk foods, fast foods and processed foods, the growth of obesity and obesity-related illness, together with continuing, possibly increasing, hunger and malnutrition;
11. the environmental costs of all of the above, including levels of energy use and their carbon emissions, in the ongoing "industrialization" of food farming, processing and sales, for example, the distances over which food is trucked, shipped and air-freighted from producer to consumer; and
12. resulting from all of the above, issues of the "sustainability" or otherwise of the current global food system, its continued growth or expanded reproduction along the trajectories noted.

These topical and highly charged themes are well covered in much public debate in both North and South and in a spate of publications.[3] Even simply listing these themes, which is all space permits, indicates connections with, and further developments of, what was covered earlier, in particular

- the pace of extraordinary technical change in farming and in the industries upstream and downstream of it (especially "chemicalization");
- how that change is driven by the profit and accumulation strategies of agri-input and agro-food industries (and their powerful lobbies in the formation of public policy); and
- differential effects for farming and food consumption in North and South, and how those effects are shaped by international divisions of labour and trade in agricultural commodities.

The End of Developmentalism

I noted above that a key feature of neoliberal globalization in the South is the policy "reform" agenda of trade liberalization, privatization and "rolling back the state." This was promoted by structural adjustment programs imposed by the World Bank and the International Monetary Fund (IMF) on governments subject to suddenly increasing debt burdens — another central aspect of the period since the 1970s. The move to liberalization was also initiated by some governments themselves, notably in India since the early 1990s. The new macroeconomic policy agenda thus signalled the end of the previous period of state-led development, including a decline in government and aid funding for agricultural development, especially along a small farmer path.

While it is impossible to generalize with any precision about the effects of neoliberal globalization for agriculture across the whole of the Third World, certain tendencies can be noted. First, the tendency to deepening commodity relations continues, but with much reduced levels of state investment, direction and control — not least the reduction or removal of direct and indirect subsidies, especially to small farmers, "perhaps the most pernicious aspect of structurally adjusted agriculture," according to Annette Desmarais (2007: 48; also emphasized by Bello 2009). In this respect, the impact of neoliberal globalization on farming tends to affect smaller and poorer farmers in the South negatively, in many areas generating new waves of "de-agrarianization" or "de-peasantization" (see chapters 6 and 7).

Second, pursuing "national development"' through industrialization and production for the domestic market ("import substitution") is abandoned where deemed "uncompetitive" in world market terms, determined by import liberalization, i.e., if a commodity can be imported at a lower price than produced domestically. The domestic market orientation of "developmentalism" is replaced by further promotion of export production according to ostensible "comparative advantage." Examples of this include the following:

- expanding "traditional" export crops like coffee, cocoa, tea, sugar, cotton and palm oil (in some cases "rehabilitating" their cultivation);
- promoting high-value commodities, especially horticultural products like fresh fruits, vegetables and cut flowers, as well as aquacultural products like prawns, typically air-freighted to the supermarkets of North America and Europe; and
- expanding large-scale production of soy, sugar and grains, some of it for biofuel production, and of livestock, notably in parts of Latin America.

Third, as these examples suggest, the deepening commodification and specialization of agricultural commodity production is undertaken by different kinds of farmers in different places: from "family" farmers to medium and large capitalist farmers, and in some cases corporate farming enterprises.

The End of the Peasantry?

The end of the "peasant," or small-scale or family farmer has been announced — and hotly contested — in different places at different times for two centuries or more. It is contested empirically: has it happened or not? where? to what extent? It is contested analytically:

why has it happened or not? has it happened to different degrees in different places? And it is contested normatively: is the end of the peasantry necessary for modern economic development, hence a good thing or a bad thing?

"Peasant elimination" (Kitching 2001) is considered a necessity by those who adhere to conceptions of capitalist and/or socialist modernization, including many Marxists, for whom it is thus a good thing, however painful. The gains of progress towards modernity, they believe, always involve major upheaval. The view that the creation of the new entails the destruction of the old was central to Marx's analysis of the development of capitalism, for all its suffering, that he described so vividly (he was also averse to romanticizing what preceded capitalism).

The view that "peasant elimination" is a bad thing is associated with populism. As Gavin Kitching (1982) showed so well, populist ideas are a recurring response to the massive social upheavals that have marked the development of capitalism throughout the history of the modern world. Advocacy of the intrinsic value and interests of the small producer, both artisan and peasant, as emblematic of "the people," arises time and again as an ideology and movement of opposition to the changes wrought by the accumulation of capital. This is the case in both the original centres of accumulation (northwestern Europe, North America) and those other regions exposed to the effects of capitalist development through their integration in its expanding world economy, from nineteenth-century Russia to the South of today. Agrarian populism, in particular, is the defence of peasant or family farmers against the threats to their reproduction by capitalism and its class agents — from merchants and banks to capitalist landed property, agrarian capital and agribusiness — and once by projects of state-led "national development" in all their capitalist, nationalist and socialist variants, of which the Soviet collectivization of agriculture in the 1930s was the most potent landmark.

Harriet Friedmann (2006: 462) refers to "the present massive assault on the remaining peasant formations of the world" (which builds on previous waves of assault), and Philip McMichael (2006: 476) observes that the "'corporate food regime'... dispossess[es] farmers as a condition for the consolidation of corporate agriculture" — an example of what Harvey (2005) terms "accumulation by dispossession" (in effect, a new wave of primitive accumulation). Recalling the discussion in chapters 2 and 3, the question can be formulated like this: does the ongoing, and intensifying, commodification of subsistence in current conditions of globalization culminate in the loss of access to land and the end of small-scale farming, more comprehensively than in the past? Does globalization represent a kind of climax of a world-historical process of "peasant elimination," which until now has proceeded unevenly and incompletely across the different times and places of the history of capitalism?

Farshad Araghi (2009) proposes a bold framework for considering such questions within the following periods:

1492–1832: "the era of colonial enclosures and the original primitive accumulation of capital in England," marked at its two ends by the arrival of Columbus in the Caribbean and the *Poor Law Amendment Act* in Britain, which signified "the beginning of a systematic attempt by the English liberal industrial bourgeoisie to dismantle the... rudimentary welfare system" (2009: 120). The purpose was to discipline the working class, just as the same industrial bourgeoisie asserted its strength against the British "agricultural interest" in the repeal of the Corn Laws fourteen years later (chapter 4 above).

1832–1917: "the food regime of capital," marking the emergence and then dominance of industrial capitalism and the global divisions of labour it created. The "agrarian policy of the colonial-liberal globalism of this period was... depeasantization, proletarianization and urbanization at home, and peasantization, ruralization and the superexploitation of coerced labour in the colonies" (122).

1917–1975, established at its two ends by the Bolshevik revolution and the victory of the Vietnamese national liberation struggle, and characterized as a period of "global reformist retreat from classical liberalism" (122), including the developmental state (of which the U.S.S.R. was the first major example).

1970s onward: neoliberal globalization, during which "the relative depeasantization and displacement of the postwar period gave way to absolute depeasantization and displacement" through a wave of "global enclosures" (133–4).

I summarize Araghi's framework here because it offers comparisons and contrasts with the historical outline used in this book and because of his conclusion that "global depeasantization is not a completed or self-completing process leading to the death of the peasantry. Social classes do not simply end and die; they live and are transformed through social struggles" (138). This brings us to examining the meaning of terms like peasantry, or small or family farmers, and to inquire more deeply into whether or not they constitute a social class and the implications of different answers to that question. Chapter 6 revisits issues and ideas concerning the persistence of peasants or family farmers in modern capitalism to this day. Chapter 7 goes more deeply into issues and ideas about class formation in the countryside. And chapter 8 explores some of the complexities of class analysis, with special reference to moving from the economic sociology of class relations to the political sociology of class action.

Notes

1. On the analogy of Roosevelt's New Deal in the U.S. in the 1930s (chapter 4), that is, with a key role for public investment, hence planning, in stimulating and shaping economic growth.
2. The GATT was founded in 1947 to reduce barriers to international trade; it was replaced in 2004 by the World Trade Organization (WTO).
3. For example, and of varying quality, Desmarais (2007), Weis (2007), Patel (2007), van der Ploeg (2008), Albritton (2009) and Bello (2009), all highly critical of corporate agriculture and advocating the alternative of a small farmer path (see chapters 7 and 8).

Chapter 6

Capitalist Agriculture and Non-Capitalist Farmers?

I have mentioned the uneven development of capitalism several times so far. In this chapter, I outline various explanations of why the development of capitalism in farming is especially uneven, with special reference to issues of the survival or persistence of peasants, or family farmers. Such explanations must always be tested in relation to particular historical conditions; as those conditions change, so can the relevance of the explanation, as I shall illustrate. The following three broad explanations have been suggested:

- "obstacles" to the investment of capital in farming;
- the interests of capital in allowing, or encouraging, the reproduction of small-scale farming; and
- resistance by small-scale farmers to dispossession and proletarianization (signalled by Araghi's reference to "social struggles" at the end of chapter 5).

"Obstacles" to Capitalist Farming
Technical Conditions of Production: Capital's "Problem" with Nature

One group of explanations suggests factors that inhibit capital from investing more generally, and more directly, in farming than in other types of production. For example, while manufacturing transforms materials already appropriated from nature (as do agri-input and agro-food industries), farming transforms nature through the very activities of appropriating it. Hence farming confronts the uncertainties of natural environments and ecological processes and how they affect the growth of plant and animal organisms.

A second explanation concerning the peculiar natural conditions of farming centres on the difference between labour time and production time (Mann and Dickinson 1978). In farming, unlike industrial production, production time exceeds labour time (in soil preparation, planting, weeding, etc) because it has to allow for the natural growth rhythms of plants and animals. This means that capital is "tied up" and unable to realize a profit before a crop is harvested or animals are ready for slaughter. However, as indicated in chapter 5, a characteristic tendency of modern capitalist agriculture is to try to bring farming in line with industrial production: to *simplify*, *standardize* and *speed up* its natural processes as much as possible. Technological innovation in farming, driven by agri-input industries in particular but also by agro-food industries, aims to produce yields of both plant and animal material that are more predictable as well as larger and faster maturing, by acting on soils (fertilizers), weeds (herbicides) and parasites (pesticides); climate (irrigation, greenhouses); plant characteristics (genetic engineering, artificial ripening); and animal growth (concentrated feeds, hormonal growth stimulants, genetic engineering).

For critics of modern capitalist agriculture, such innovations represent an ever more intense "industrialization" of farming with serious and mounting ecological costs — including health costs as a result of how food is grown and processed and the declining nutritional value and rising toxicity levels of many foods. Following are two examples, among many possible. One is the ecological shift of field crop cultivation over the last 150 years — and which is intensifying all the time — from historical "closed-loop agro-ecosystems" (chapter 4), with their complex interactions of soil and plant chemistry and micro-organisms, to the radical simplification of systems based on increasing applications of fertilizers and other chemicals. In the latter, the soil becomes merely a medium for the absorption of chemicals to "flow through" into the faster growth of more plants with higher yields. This results in sterile soils that require ever more chemicals to grow anything; the intensity of "'chemicalization" in turn adds toxicity to soils (and to watersheds), the plants that grow in them and the food we eat.

A second example is that of "confined animal feeding operations," used to produce as much beef, pork and chicken in as concentrated a space as possible in as short a time as possible. Indeed, this is also a kind of "flow-through" system, in which the body of the animal is the medium that absorbs concentrated feeds and hormonal growth stimulants, along with high levels of antibiotics to counter the risks of disease among closely confined animals. Poultry production is perhaps the most striking example of industrialized agriculture, because a standardized chicken "factory," with its enclosed and controlled environment, is completely mobile. It can be established anywhere that is profitable, thus "liberating" capital from land and locale specific constraints,, which characterized the whole history of farming until now.[1]

Social Dynamics of Production:
Rent, Labour Process, Labour Costs

Certain social dynamics of production can also present obstacles to capitalist farming. One explanation suggests that the burden of ground rent as a deduction from profit encourages capital to leave "family" farmers to absorb its costs (Djurfeldt 1981), in the same way that they absorb risk and the delayed realization of the value of agricultural commodities. Another obstacle concerns the labour process: it is much more difficult, hence costly, to supervise and control the pace and quality of work in the field or orchard than it is in the factory, which gives an advantage to family labour over wage labour in farming. Third, when rapid industrialization and its associated urbanization raise wage rates, family farms can enjoy a "labour-price advantage" over capitalist farms, a factor in "the failure of agrarian capitalism" — or, rather, capitalist farming — in Britain, Germany, the Netherlands and the U.S. from 1846 to 1919, according to Niek Koning (1994).

The above explanations can also be interpreted from a different perspective. They might be seen as ways in which small-scale farming is *competitive*, in the sense that small farmers absorb costs and risks that capitalist farmers are unwilling to bear. Hence, depending on circumstances, small-scale farmers might be able to supply agricultural commodities more cheaply than capitalist farmers, who might find it more profitable to invest in agricultural activities upstream and downstream. This brings us to the second set of explanations of the unevenness of capitalist development in farming, namely the benefits to capital of leaving farming to "family" farmers.

Exploitation: The Benefits of "Family Farming" to Capital?

As noted, the benefits of "family" farming to capital might simply be the other side of the coin of "obstacles" to capitalist farming, albeit "obstacles" that are not immutable but that capital tries to shift. I also indicated that ideas about benefits to capital hinge on the proposition that small-scale farming is competitive with capitalist farming. Here I want to clarify some ambiguities and complexities in how those ideas are formulated and applied, not least in relation to the social character of the *labour* employed in "family" farming, hence issues of *exploitation*.

In the 1920s, the great Russian agricultural economist A.V. Chayanov (1888–1937), wrote:

> In the most developed capitalist countries, such as those in North America, widely developed mortgage credit, the financing of farm circulating capital, and the dominating part played by capital invested in transport, elevator, irrigation, and other undertakings... [represent] new ways in which capitalism penetrates agriculture. These ways convert the farmer into a labor force working with other people's means of production. They convert agriculture, despite the evident scattered and independent nature of the small commodity producers, into an economic system concentrated in a series of the largest undertakings and, through them, entering the sphere controlled by the most advanced forms of finance capitalism. (1966: 202)

This is a remarkable statement for its time. Note, first, Chayanov's potent suggestion that the "economic system" of modern capitalist agriculture extends beyond agri-input and agro-food industries to control "by the most advanced forms of finance capitalism," which can apply to land markets and trade in agricultural commodities, often highly speculative activities, as well as farmers' production credit. Second, Chayanov refers to apparently independent (family) farmers as "small commodity producers" (what I have called petty commodity producers). Third, he implies that in modern capitalist agriculture, such farmers are not "independent" at all but occupy the class place of labour in relation to capital: "a labor force working with other people's means of production." Hence farmers are exploited in the same sense as labour is exploited by capital more generally, albeit in a different form — and presumably for as long as this benefits capital.

Chayanov assumed that the farmers in question are "*small commodity producers*" whose farms are worked with family (or household) labour without the employment of wage labour. This assumption is a limiting one, theoretically and historically, for several reasons concerning scale, notions of "the family farm" and relations with capital upstream and downstream of farming. First, in Chayanov's time, scale was still largely measured by farm *size* — implicitly the area of land that could be worked with family labour using the means of production then available. In modern capitalism, a more relevant measure of scale is farm *capitalization*: the amounts of capital required to establish different types of farming — their "entry costs" in economists' terms — and to reproduce them. This can have effects for farm size, of course, when mechanization makes it possible for relatively few workers to cultivate a far larger area, as in grain and oilseed production. On the other hand, some of the most productive branches of horticulture — fresh fruit and vegetables, orchards and vineyards, and flowers — contain enterprises that are relatively small in land area but highly capitalized and labour intensive.

Second, the notion of the "family farm" is often used to refer variously to family-*owned*, family-*managed* or family-*worked* farms, which can be misleading. A family-owned farm can be a fully capitalist enterprise run by a hired farm manager and worked by wage labour. Similarly, a family-managed farm can be a capitalist enterprise employing wage workers and/or hiring specialized contractors for ploughing, planting, crop spraying and harvesting (as in some American grain farms). This leaves the family-worked farm, which provides the strongest meaning of a "family" farm and the only instance in which exploitation of the farmer, in any meaningful sense, might be possible. I come back to this issue below, while noting for the moment that enterprises designated as family-worked farms often employ wage labour as well.

Third, the farms that tend to be most fully incorporated in

modern capitalist agriculture, as described by Chaynaov for North America — for example, those that supply agro-food corporations on contracts that specify exactly their "inputs, production processes and outputs" (Albritton 2009: 82) — are usually capitalist enterprises employing wage labour. In this respect they are not different from often small capitalist enterprises that specialize in producing, say, vehicle components on contract to large automobile manufacturers. The owners of such agricultural enterprises, "farmers," cannot be "exploited" by the corporations they contract with or the banks they borrow from (even though they often claim that they are!); rather they exploit the workers they employ (as explained in chapter 2).

Chayanov had another concept of exploitation, which is better known and widely used in "peasant studies," namely *"self-exploitation."* This derives from his argument that the imperatives of reproduction in family-labour farms mean that additional labour costs are discounted in adverse conditions. The household does not calculate the costs of its own labour in farming its land in the way that capitalist farmers have to incorporate wage costs in their calculations of expenditure and expected profit. In effect, "peasants" tend to farm more intensively than capitalists, albeit at lower levels of labour productivity; similarly they are often constrained to buy or rent land at higher prices and to sell their product at lower prices than capitalist farmers are prepared to do.

The idea that small family farmers can bear costs of production and reproduction, including lower levels of consumption— thereby exploiting themselves — than capitalist farmers are prepared to accept is not unique or original to Chayanov. It features in other explanations of the apparent staying power of small-scale farming — or "persistence of the peasantry" — throughout the era of modern capitalism, including that by the Marxist Karl Kautsky (1988) at the end of the nineteenth century. The argument is that this staying power or "persistence" is tolerated, and even encouraged, by capital as long as peasant or family farming can continue to produce "cheap" food commodities that lower the costs of labour power (wages) to capitalists, and indeed itself produces "cheap" labour power. That is, peasants and small farmers who also sell their labour power can be paid less because their wage does not have to cover the full costs of household reproduction, which are partly met through its farming — sometimes seen as a "subsidy" to the capitals that employ rural labour migrants. There were glimpses of this in colonial conditions described in chapter 3 on "semi-proletarianization," and I consider it further in chapter 7.

To summarize this brief survey so far: various arguments in political economy seek to explain why the evolution of capitalist agriculture has not comprehensively generated capitalist farming. A common theme in those explanations is that capitalist agriculture devises ways of subsuming or incorporating small or family farmers (or "peasants") within its market structures and dynamics of accumulation, as long as this provides benefits to capital. This is often, if not necessarily, associated with some notion that farmers are "exploited" by capital, directly or indirectly, whether in the South ("peasants") or in the North, where farmers' share of the total value of agricultural output has been in steady decline, relative to the increasing shares of inputs (and their costs), which benefit agri-input corporations, and of processing and marketing, which accrue to agro-food corporations (Weis 2007: 82).

Finally, we should recognize that small farmers in some regions of the South were largely "by-passed" by capitalism's penetration of agriculture, in Chayanov's terms, sometimes for long periods.[2] The "persistence of the peasantry" might reflect the fact that primitive accumulation is uneven and protracted, even if it is now being completed in some places through an intensified "accumulation by dispossession," as some argue (chapter 5). In short, such processes are contingent and subject to change. This was also signalled by the view that capitalism devises ways of subsuming small-scale farmers as long as this provides benefits to capital. But is it enough to attribute change exclusively to the interests of capital? What of the "social struggles" that Araghi refers to?

The Role of Resistance

Many scholars conceive of the uneven development of farming in capitalism, including its colonial periods in the South, as histories of *resistance* by small farmers and peasants to commodification, dispossession and proletarianization. Such resistance is manifested in struggles over land, rent, taxes, debt, forced cultivation, labour conscription and control that colonial and independent states sought to impose on small farmers in the name of progress — whether the mission of colonialism to "civilize" peoples of colour (chapter 3), or "modernize" agriculture as a strategy for economic development (chapter 4). There are many examples of such resistance on larger and smaller, heroic and mundane scales. The heroic scale is exemplified in Eric Wolf's book *Peasant Wars of the Twentieth Century* (1969), with its case studies of Mexico, Russia, China, Vietnam, Algeria and Cuba from the 1900s to the 1960s.[3] In today's conditions, it is expressed in the belief that neoliberal globalization has generated a counter-movement of "global agrarian resistance" (McMichael, 2006).[4]

The smaller scale is exemplified by James C. Scott's *Weapons of the Weak* (1985), a study of a village in Malaysia in the late 1970s. Scott argued provocatively that the continuous and cumulative effects of "everyday forms of peasant resistance" within socially differentiated rural localities do more to improve the conditions of peasant farmers than occasional, more widely recognized, episodes of conflict and rebellion.[5] But is it useful to replace a one-sided emphasis on the interests, and presumed omnipotence, of capital with a similarly one-sided narrative of resistance, on various scales from the heroic to the mundane?

In colonial conditions, colonial states were often not prepared to take on the massive task of dispossessing peasantries, especially in densely populated countrysides, with all the upheaval and disorder that would entail. Rather, as we saw in chapter 3, they embarked on measures which led, directly and indirectly, intentionally or unintentionally, to the commodification of peasant subsistence. This was facilitated by incorporating or adapting indigenous hierarchies — "older [pre-colonial] structures of power" (Bagchi 2009: 87) — in their systems of rural administration, including control of land: *caciques* in Latin America, *zamindars* in northern India, "tribal" chiefs in sub-Saharan Africa (Mamdani, 1996). In India and Africa, colonial states sometimes also sought to promote a "yeomanry," a class of petty capitalist farmers, from the ranks of the peasantry.

The colonial project, and its impact on indigenous peasantries, was often shaped and constrained by its own contradictions. For example, Michael Cowen and Robert Shenton (1991a, 1991b) argue that British colonialism in Africa aimed to deliver economic progress without social and political disruption. This meant gradually introducing its African subjects to the production and consumption of commodities, the material basis of bourgeois civilization, while maintaining social order by "customary" means: reinforcing rural "community," "tribal" identity and patriarchal and chiefly authority. Accordingly, Africans were not to be allowed any immediate enjoyment of such bourgeois rights as private title in land and access to bank credit. In Cowen and Shenton's view, this held back the fuller development of capitalism, from which Africans would have benefitted more.

Finally, some colonial peasants themselves initiated new paths of specialized commodity production. Polly Hill's (1963), study of migrant cocoa farmers of Southern Ghana (cited in chapter 3), provides a well-known example of the self-transformation of "subsistence" farmers into commodity producers. Moreover, Hill was clear that over time the more successful of them became capitalist farmers. More generally, rather than simply being either passive victims or active opponents of colonial imposition, many peasants tried to *negotiate* the shift towards commodity production (commodification of subsistence) they confronted, in more or less favourable circumstances, mobilizing larger or smaller resources of land and labour, with greater or lesser success. The same applies to responses to the impositions of "national development" following independence from colonial rule.

With political independence and the period of "developmentalism," there were deliberate strategies to promote small farmer development along the lines of modernization and further commodification. Some of the policies to achieve this were noted in chapter 4. Here I consider another policy of great significance (hence also hotly contested), which was mentioned in chapter 5, namely redistributive *land reform*. This concludes the analytical exposition of this chapter and connects it with the next.

The Case of Land Reforms

Land reforms have marked some of the key moments of modern history from the French Revolution in the late eighteenth century onwards. The redistribution of property rights in land can take very different forms, including

- the confiscation of larger farms and estates and their subdivision among small farmers;
- conferring ownership of land they already farm on small farmers, to free them from the exactions of rent and landowners' authority and to give them more secure tenure;
- the nationalization or socialization of large commercial farms and plantations; and
- the decollectivization of state farms and communes in the former Soviet bloc, China, Vietnam and Cuba.

Land reforms are always political processes, albeit often with an economic rationale and always with socioeconomic consequences. The first two kinds are associated with the potent slogan, "land to the tiller," which features in land reforms both "from below" and "from above." In land reforms from below, peasant political action against poverty, hunger, social injustice and oppression played a major part. They culminated with particular intensity from about 1900 to the 1970s: in Mexico and Russia in the 1910s, eastern and southern Europe and China in the inter-war period (continuing in China into the 1940s and 1950s) and Bolivia in the 1950s, Vietnam and Algeria in the 1950s and 1960s, Peru in the 1960s, and Mozambique and Nicaragua in the 1970s and 1980s. Struggles against large landed property and its social power were especially intense when they combined with anti-colonial or anti-imperialist struggles.

In some instances, land reform from above in the post-war period was a response to the "threat" of social upheaval represented by "peasant wars" and social revolution, for example, in Italy, Japan and Korea in the 1940s and 1950s under U.S. military occupation, and in the U.S.-led Alliance for Progress in Latin America in the 1960s, following the Cuban revolution. In other instances, land reforms from above were initiated by modernizing regimes of varying nationalist complexions between the 1950s and 1970s: from Nehru's independent India and Nasser's Egypt to the Iran of the last Shah.

Land reform from above largely disappeared from the agenda of agricultural and development policy after the 1970s but returned in the 1990s, now reinvented as market-based reform on the principle of "willing seller, willing buyer." This is how the International Fund for Agricultural Development put it: "Previous land reforms have been unduly confiscatory, statist or top-down. 'New wave' land reform, which is decentralised, *market-friendly* and involves civil society action or consensus, is sometimes feasible and consistent with just and durable property rights' (IFAD 2001: 75, emphasis added).

The economic rationale of land reform from above is that small farmers with secure possession of land and the right incentives will increase productivity, unlike those large landowners who leave land idle, use it for speculation or appropriate rents that they fail to reinvest in farm production. Hence land reform from above does not aim to divide capitalist farms that are commercially successful, as they represent agricultural modernization. This was indicated by a former minister of land reform in the Christian Democrat government of Eduardo Frei in Chile in the 1960s:

> A certain proportion of the new peasant beneficiaries [of land reform] will probably *fail as entrepreneurs*... It will be necessary to caution against too rigid an institutional link between the beneficiaries and the land so that a *natural selection* may take place later which will *allow those who fail to be eliminated.* (Chonchol 1970: 160, emphases added)

Some "modernizing" land reforms have accelerated the pace of capitalist development in farming, as Chonchol recommended, while in many cases the poorest categories of the rural population obtained less land than richer "peasants" and embryonic capitalist farmers. This was the case in India, Egypt, Iran and much of Latin America, for example, especially for women farmers and agricultural wage workers, who generally have the weakest land rights. In his magisterial work on India, written in the 1960s, Swedish economist

Gunnar Myrdal argued that land reforms after independence "bolstered the political, social, and economic position of the rural upper strata on which the present government depends for crucial support" (1968: 1387). Myrdal is cited by historian David Low (1996: 25), who extends the argument to Iran, Egypt and across much of Asia and Africa.

Conclusion

What does this brief and selective overview of land reform add to issues considered in this chapter?

First, it provides a further example of how important political dynamics can be in the "persistence" of small-scale farming in capitalism.

Second, it makes clear that the economic rationale of land reform from above is to establish small farmers as viable commodity producers, "entrepreneurs," in Chonchol's term, who are competitive and able to hold their own in markets. This connects with one of the main themes of the next chapter.

Third, the issue of who benefits from land reforms of different kinds also connects with the questions addressed in chapter 7 concerning class formation among farmers.

Notes

1. Brazil, Thailand and China together doubled their share of world trade in poultry from 23 percent in 1995 to 46 percent in 2003 (Burch 2003).
2. This does not mean that they were "by-passed" by commodity relations, as I explain in chapter 7.
3. The seminal work by Barrington Moore Jr (1966) compared the role of class struggles between landed property and peasants in state formation in seventeenth-century England, eighteenth-century France, nineteenth-century U.S. (the American Civil War and subsequent abolition of slavery as "the last capitalist revolution") and nineteenth- and twentieth-century China, Japan and India (the only colonial example).
4. The concept of "counter-movements" to unregulated capitalist development comes from the famous work of Karl Polanyi (1957).
5. Hence Scott (2005) is also sceptical of claims about a contemporary "global agrarian resistance," on which see chapter 8 below.

Chapter 7

Class Formation in the Countryside

Do "family farmers" in the South ("peasants") constitute a social "class," as many assert? And, as some suggest, does this "class" also incorporate family farmers in the North? The general basis of this view is that these farmers represent family-labour enterprises engaged in simple reproduction ("subsistence") and that they have certain common values and virtues (noted in the Introduction). Those who "take the part of family farmers" usually emphasize their desire for autonomy: to farm in ways they value and that are socially equitable and environmentally friendly (including reconstructing local food economies); hence their resistance to today's relentless pressures of globalization on agriculture.[1]

Can we identify a class, in any useful sense, by an aspiration or set of values? In the political economy presented in this book, class is based in social relations of production. As such, a class can only be identified through its relations with another class. For some agrarian populists (chapter 5), "family farmers" are also considered a class by virtue of their relations with capital, as "exploited" by capital in some sense. Chapter 6 uncovered several possible meanings of capitalist exploitation of *family labour* (as distinct from wage labour) in farming: as a labour force working with other people's means of production or as self-exploiting in ways that represent indirect exploitation by capital or at least in ways that benefit capital.[2]

Some scholars see family farmers in the South as a class historically exploited by capital and the state and central to accumulation during the periods of colonialsim and developmentalism (chapter 4), but which is now subject to *dispossession,* or "global depeasantization," in Araghi's term (chapter 5). Dispossession or marginalization implies that diminishing numbers of small farmers are available for "exploitation," presumably because capital (or capitalist agriculture) no longer needs them.

In this chapter I explore whether family farmers plausibly constitute a single exploited "class" or are themselves differentiated into classes. I do this first in terms of the relations and dynamics of *commodification, petty commodity production* and *differentiation*, and then of *classes of labour* in capitalism. All these concepts have been mentioned previously in the text and are brought together and examined further here, in a sequence that adds more complexity at each step. I introduce further "determinations" to explore theoretically the sources and forms of such complexity in the real world.

The Class Dynamics of "Family Farming"

Commodification

Commodification is the process through which the elements of production and social reproduction are produced for, and obtained from, market exchange and subjected to its disciplines and compulsions. In capitalism, this process is premised on the historical emergence and formation of a fundamental social relation between capital and wage labour. The central tendency of capitalism towards generalized commodity production does not mean that all elements of social existence are necessarily and comprehensively commodified. Rather it signifies the commodification of subsistence: that *reproduction cannot take place outside commodity relations* and the disciplines they impose (Marx's "dull compulsion of economic forces").

Of course, processes of the commodification of small-scale farming display massive variation. While for Marx — and for many others, like Karl Polanyi (1957) — the enclosure of land and its conversion into private property was the decisive moment in primitive accumulation in England (chapter 2), there can be other sequences of commodification of the elements of production and reproduction. For example, one kind of colonial sequence was the commodification of, first, crops — typically as a result of "forced commercialization" to begin with — then some means of consumption, then tools and other instruments of labour, then labour itself (as the commodity labour power) and only finally land (the object of labour). Legally constituted and enforced private property rights in land are still not established effectively, and are resisted and contested, in some rural zones in the South. This, however, is not a barrier to the development of commodity relations in farming, as suggested by "vernacular markets" in land, that is, land treated as private property in practice (*de facto*) if not in law (*de jure*). In fact, vibrant vernacular markets in land are typically found in areas of dynamic agricultural petty, and not so petty, commodity production (Chimhowu and Woodhouse 2006).

Petty Commodity Production
Petty commodity production in capitalism combines the class "places," or locations, of both capital and labour: in farming, capital in the form of land, tools, seeds, fertilizers and other chemicals, and labour in the form of families/households. It is a "contradictory unity" of class places for several reasons. First, those class places are not distributed evenly within farming households, especially given gender divisions of property, labour, income and spending, as suggested by the Tanzanian vignette in the Introduction. Second, there is a contradiction between reproducing the means of production (capital) and reproducing the producer (labour). In the terms used in chapter 1, this concerns the distribution of income (including from borrowing) between, on one hand, the replacement fund and fund of rent and, on the other hand, the funds for consumption and generational reproduction — a distribution that is usually strongly gendered. Third, the contradictory combination of class places is the source of differentiation of petty commodity enterprises, which I consider in a moment.

This approach contrasts with the misleading assumption, less common today than in the past, that small farmers in the South are "subsistence" cultivators whose primary objective is to supply their food needs from their own farming. Beyond securing that objective, any involvement in markets is seen as discretionary, a matter of choice — what I call the "subsistence plus" model. I argue that once farming households are integrated in capitalist commodity relations, they are subject to the dynamics and compulsions of commodification, which are *internalized* in their relations and practices. If they farm only for their own consumption, this is because they are integrated in commodity relations in other ways, usually through the sale of their labour power. In this case, it is common for "subsistence" production to be funded from wages, which are also used to buy food when own-account farming is inadequate to supply household needs, whether on a regular basis or in bad harvest years. In effect, this turns "subsistence plus" on its head: the extent to which "small farmers" can satisfy their food needs from their own production is shaped by the ways they are integrated in commodity relations.

Class Differentiation

In chapter 3, I suggested that by the end of the colonial period, from the 1940s in Asia and late 1950s in Africa, and earlier in Latin America, small farmers or peasants were "locked into" commodity production by the "dull compulsion of economic forces": the commodification of their subsistence. Once this is the case, there is a tendency of differentiation into classes that Lenin (1964a) termed rich, middle and poor peasants:

- those able to accumulate productive assets and reproduce themselves as capital on a larger scale, engaging in *expanded reproduction*, are emergent capitalist farmers, corresponding to Lenin's "rich peasants";
- those able to reproduce themselves as capital on the same scale of production, and as labour on the same scale of consumption (and generationally) — what Marx termed *simple reproduction* — are medium farmers, corresponding to Lenin's "middle peasants"; and
- those struggling to reproduce themselves as capital, hence struggling to reproduce themselves as labour from their own farming and subject to what I term a *simple reproduction squeeze*, are poor farmers, corresponding to Lenin's "poor peasants."

Emergent capitalist farmers tend to employ wage labour in addition to, or in place of, family labour. Poor farmers experience most acutely the contradiction of reproducing themselves as both labour and capital and may reduce their consumption to extreme levels in order to retain possession of a small piece of land or a cow, to buy seeds or to repay debts. As Chayanov (1991: 40) put it: "In the course of the most ferocious economic struggle for existence, the ... [small farmer] who knows how to starve is the one who is best adapted."

Medium farmers, especially those who are relatively stable petty commodity producers, are of special interest, not least because they are dear to the heart of agrarian populism (chapter 6) and indeed to the "yeoman farmer" ideal of some colonial administrations. This sometimes reflects an assumption that the "middle peasant" condition was the norm in rural communities before capitalism, which are regarded, rather romantically, as intrinsically egalitarian. Consequently, the emergence of rich and poor peasants is seen as an unfortunate deviation, a kind of fall from grace, caused by malevolent forces external to peasant communities.

The theoretical schema proposed here recommends a different view: that medium farmers are also produced by class differentiation. Processes of commodification raise the "entry" costs (chapter 6) and reproduction costs of capital in farming, and the risks associated with those higher costs, and increase competition for land and/or the labour to work it. Thus, even "medium" family farmers establish their commodity enterprises at the expense of their neighbours who are poorer farmers, unable to meet those costs or bear those risks and losing out to those who can. They are likely to be forced out of farming or, if they can obtain credit, become highly indebted and slide towards marginal farming (as defined in the Introduction).

India's Green Revolution provides a clue to this aspect of differentiation. The promise was that its biochemical package of improved inputs was "scale neutral," meaning that it could be adopted, with benefit, on any size of farm — unlike mechanization, for instance, which requires minimum economies of scale. However, "scale neutral" — an attribute of a given technology — is not the same as "resource neutral," a social attribute connected with the question "who owns what?" and that requires asking about differentiation and its effects. As John Harriss (1987: 321) explained in relation to the adoption of the Green Revolution package in India: "The crucial point here is that those disposing of more resources are in a much better position to cope with the risks associated with this higher cash-intensity technology."[3]

Marginal farmers, or those "too poor to farm," do not necessarily lack access to land but they do lack one or more of the following to be able to reproduce themselves through their own farming:

- enough land of good enough quality;
- the capacity to buy other necessary means of production, like tools and seeds; and
- the capacity to command adequate labour, often an effect of gender relations that prevent women farmers commanding the labour of men.

Class differentiation of farmers as petty commodity producers involves other factors and complexities too. For example, rural labour markets are a critical condition of petty commodity production in farming, however common it is to overlook the employment of wage labour by even "small" farmers. In the contemporary European context, for example, Toby Shelley (2007: 1) observes: "France prides itself on its self-sufficient peasant agriculture, yet without Moroccan field workers many farmers would struggle."[4] And in an excellent study of rural Costa Rica in the 1980s, Marc Edelman (1999: 122, 123, 167) refers to "peasant" hiring of labourers, or *peons*, and reports that small farmers complained about their lack of cash to hire *peons*, although he does not say who those *peons* were nor where they came from in the rural class structure.

Another general theme, or hypothesis, of even wider scope is that the practices, fortunes and prospects of farmers are increasingly shaped by their activities outside their farms and the incomes those activities provide for their consumption funds (reproduction as labour) and investment funds (reproduction as capital). Frank Ellis (1998: 10) notes: "Non-farm income sources are beyond doubt critical for describing the living standards of farm households in developing countries." This rural "livelihood diversification" connects with tendencies to class differentiation, which it might intensify or impede, according to circumstances.

Emergent capitalist farmers often invest in activities ancillary to farming, like crop trading and processing, rural retail trade and transport, advancing credit, renting out draft animals and tractors and selling irrigation water. They also invest in urban activities, education for their sons and good marriages for their daughters, and alliances with government officials, and in political processes and influence more generally. In short, they engage in "diversification for accumulation" (Hart 1994).

Medium-scale farming typically rests on combining farming with off-farm activities, including labour migration, as a source of income to help reproduce farm production, especially when its costs of reproduction are rising. It also rests, as just noted, on the capacity to hire wage labour, provided by landless workers or marginal farmers, who are often migrants. Wage labour may be hired to replace family labour engaged in other off-farm activities or to augment family labour at moments of peak demand in the farming calendar, like weeding and harvesting.

Poor or marginal farmers engage in "survival" activities to reproduce themselves, primarily through the sale of their labour power. This is acknowledged, however belatedly, by organizations like the IFAD and the World Bank. The IFAD's *Rural Poverty Report 2001* notes that the rural poor "live mainly by selling their labour-power" (2001: 230), and Table 7.1 is adapted from the *World Development Report 2008* (World Bank 2007: 205).

The table suggests that own-account farming is the primary economic activity for more than half the adult rural population only in sub-Saharan Africa. However, a strong trend of "de-agrarianization" or "de-peasantization" (Bryceson 1999) has been argued for sub-Saharan Africa, manifested in the growing proportion of rural incomes derived from non-farm sources. Moreover, the comprehen-

Table 7.1 Share of Adult Rural Population with Own Account Farming as Primary Economic Activity (%)

Region	Men	Women
Sub-Saharan Africa	56.6	53.5
South Asia	33.1	12.7
East Asia and Pacific (excluding China)	46.8	38.4
Middle East and North Africa	24.6	38.6
Europe and Central Asia	8.5	6.9
Latin America and the Caribbean	38.4	22.8

sive economic crisis that has gripped most of sub-Saharan Africa in recent decades puts additional pressures on reproduction through longstanding combinations of farming and labour migration, of "hoe and wage," in the term of Cordell et al. (1996). This is because opportunities in urban employment (including "informal" employment and self-employment), which can provide sources of support to farming in the countryside, have declined at the same time as pressures on most farming households have increased, in large part as a result of neoliberal globalization (chapter 5).

A further factor that complicates class formation is that the precarious conditions of small-scale farming in the South exert pressures on the reproduction of farming households. Medium farmers are often pushed into the ranks of poor farmers because of their vulnerability to "shocks" like drought, flood and deteriorating terms of exchange between what they need to buy and what they are able to sell — a typical expression of the "simple reproduction squeeze." They can buy fewer "inputs" and less food and labour power when they earn less from their farming. This may be because of reduced harvests — due to adverse weather, crop diseases, pest infestations, insufficient fertilizers or labour shortages — or reduced prices for the commodities they sell or because they have to repay debts. Precariousness is also registered in the vulnerability of *individual* households to "shocks," for example, the illness or death of a key household member[5] or of a valued draft animal, either of which might mean crossing the threshold between "getting by" and "going under."

Variations in Differentiation

Just as by the mid-twentieth century, small farmers in the South were "locked into" commodity relations, so were they also widely, if unevenly, differentiated in class terms. The extent of differentiation may have been inhibited by the depredations of colonialism in some regions, for example, as an effect of "parasitic landlordism" in colonial India (chapter 3) or where moneylenders and merchants exerted a strong grip on the rural economy. But differentiation on a larger or smaller scale emerged from processes of commodification and was sometimes promoted by colonial agricultural policies. Low (1996), cited in chapter 6, suggested that locally entrenched classes of richer farmers were the dominant social force in the countryside at the time of independence from colonial rule in Asia and Africa — *and* with a reach that extended beyond the countryside.

Like patterns of the commodification of small-scale farming, patterns of differentiation also display massive variation. The *tendency* to differentiation that can be identified theoretically from the contradictory unity of class places in petty commodity production is not — and cannot be — evident in identical *trends*, mechanisms, rhythms or forms of class differentiation everywhere. This is because "many determinations" (Marx) mediate between the tendency and particular concrete circumstances and local dynamics. I have indicated some of those determinations, which might appear paradoxical, for example, the centrality of off-farm income and hiring wage labour to the reproduction of medium-scale farmers, which disturbs their idealized image as the "independent" family farmer, "middle peasant" or sturdy yeoman. Similarly, the sale of their labour power by the poor can help some of them cling to a piece of land, however marginal. They often make considerable sacrifices to do so, because that land represents an element of security, and perhaps hope, in the "economic struggle for existence" (Chaynaov) they confront, as well as a marker of cultural value and identity.

Depending on circumstances, there can also be limits to expansion of their farming by richer farmers. Harriss (1987) studied a village in southeast India, where households farmed an average of 1.2 hectares of irrigated rice and groundnuts. There was inequality between households, but it was not increasing in terms of the distribution of land and scale of farming because of resistance to richer farmers acquiring more land in this densely populated and intensively cultivated area and because of inheritance practices of dividing family land between sons. Richer farmers diversified into rice trading, which was more feasible and profitable than expanding the scale of their farming.

By contrast, in the very different conditions of northern Uganda in the 1980s, a local village capitalist told Mahmood Mamdani (1987: 208): "What helped us [to accumulate] was the famine of 1980. People were hungry and they sold us things cheaply [including land and cattle]. That is when we really started buying." As always in capitalism, the crises of some present opportunities to others, a dynamic that permeates the often intricate and fluid contours of class formation in the countryside.

Classes of Labour

Teodor Shanin (1986: 19), considering the legacy of Chayanov some sixty years after his major works were published, observed: "Rural society and rural problems are inexplicable any longer in their own terms and must be understood in terms of labor and capital flows which are broader than agriculture." One dimension of this, concerning capital, is what we might call *agriculture beyond the farm*. Chapter 4 considered the distinctions in modern capitalism between farming and the "agricultural sector" in both economic and political terms. The agricultural sector can include "agrarian capital beyond the countryside," that is, investment in land and farming by urban business (including politicians, civil servants, military officers and affluent professionals) as well as by corporate agro-food capital.

The above overview of commodification, the class basis of petty commodity production and the class differentiation of "family" farmers highlights the other dimension, that of labour. We can call this *rural labour beyond the farm*, supplied not only by fully "proletarianized" rural workers who are landless, hence unable to farm on their own account, but also by marginal farmers or those too poor to farm as a major component of their livelihood and reproduction. Both categories of labour, which typically have fluid social boundaries, can be employed locally on the farms of neighbours (capitalist and petty commodity producers) or seasonally in more distant zones of capitalist farming and well-established petty commodity production, sometimes elsewhere in their own country, sometimes in another country. "Footloose labour," in the term of Jan Breman (1996), is a massive fact of social life of the rural zones of today's South and expresses the ways in which their types of farming are differentiated by class dynamics.

What I term here "classes of labour" comprise "the growing numbers... who now depend — directly *and indirectly* — on the sale of their labour power for their own daily reproduction" (Panitch and Leys 2001: ix, my emphasis). They have to pursue their reproduction in conditions of growing income insecurity and "pauperization" as well as employment insecurity and the downward pressures exerted by the neoliberal erosion of social provision for those in "standard" wage employment, who are shrinking as a proportion of classes of labour in most regions of the South, and in some instances in absolute terms as well.[6] Pressures on reproduction have even more serious consequences for the growing numbers of what Mike Davis (2006: 178) calls "the global informal working class," which "is about one billion strong, making it the fastest-growing, and most unprecedented, social class on earth."

Davis is referring to urban workers, but it is also worth considering whether poor farmers in the South are part of "the global informal working class." They might not be dispossessed of *all* means of reproducing themselves, recalling Lenin's warning against "too stereotyped an understanding of the theoretical proposition that capitalism requires the free, landless worker" (1964a: 181). But nor do most of them possess *sufficient* means to reproduce themselves, which marks the limits of their viability as petty commodity producers.

The working poor of the South have to pursue their reproduction through insecure, oppressive and typically increasingly scarce wage employment and/or a range of likewise precarious small-scale and "informal economy" survival activity, including marginal farming. In effect, livelihoods are pursued through complex *combinations* of wage employment and self-employment.[7] Additionally, many pursue their means of reproduction across different sites of the social division of labour: urban and rural, agricultural and non-agricultural, wage employment and marginal self-employment. The social locations and identities the working poor inhabit, combine and move between make for ever more fluid boundaries and defy inherited assumptions of fixed and uniform notions of "worker," "farmer," "petty trader," "urban," "rural," "employed" and "self-employed."

Relative success or failure in labour markets, salaried employment and other activities is typically key to the viability (reproduction) of agricultural petty commodity production, but it is not distributed equally across those who farm or otherwise have an interest in farming and access to land. In turn, this has effects for those in classes of labour who combine self-employment in farming and other branches of the "informal economy" with wage labour. As small-scale farmers, as well as off-farm workers, they inhabit a social world of "relentless micro-capitalism" (Davis 2006: 181).

Conclusion

For analytical purposes it is sometimes useful to think about capital in general, and I often use the term "capital" in this abstract way, for example, in referring to the interests or dynamics of capital. However, capital can be distinguished by:

- *activities and sectors*: agricultural and industrial, financial and commercial;
- *scales*: from households and "small business," including petty commodity producers in farming, to global corporations; and
- *classes of capital*: distinguished by the interests and strategies of capital in particular activities and sectors and on scales from local to regional, national to transnational.

This chapter illustrated and sought to explain further the concrete diversity of classes of capital, as well as classes of labour, in the countrysides of the South, and how that diversity is shaped by factors ("determinations") beyond the countryside, beyond farming and beyond agriculture. A variety of forms and classes of capital has been indicated, from corporate agribusiness to "rich peasants" or village capitalists, who buy up the land and livestock of their impoverished neighbours or who diversify into crop trading. In the face of such diversity and the contradictions and struggles that produce it, it is difficult to adhere to any notion of farmers — whether described as "peasants," "family farmers" or "small farmers" — as a single class and, moreover, constituted as a class through any common social relation with capital. In the final chapter I take forward some of the ideas discussed here to consider additional complexities concerning political practices and processes — the political sociology of class.

7 / CLASS FORMATION IN THE COUNTRYSIDE

Notes

1. Those farmers in the vanguard of doing so through their alternative farming practices are termed "the new peasantries" by van der Ploeg (2008).
2. A different, if usually connected, claim is that "the people of the land," comprising all "small" farmers everywhere, can become a class or acquire class-like qualities by uniting in a common political project. This is considered in the next chapter.
3. They were also often better placed to obtain the HYV packages more easily and on more preferential terms.
4. "Self-sufficient peasant agriculture" may seem a strange description of farming in France today. Indeed, Shelley is referring to a particular national, and populist, myth, in which hired labour, especially immigrant labour, vanishes from sight.
5. Especially with the HIV-AIDS pandemic adding to the health risks of rural existence in the South, particularly in some parts of Africa.
6. And whose wages often support wider networks of kin, urban and rural.
7. Concepts of "self-employment" are highly problematic and are often misleadingly applied to those who are "wage workers in thin disguise" (Harriss-White and Gooptu 2000: 96).

Chapter 8

Complexities of Class

Economic Sociology and Political Sociology

The analytical complexities and concrete variations highlighted in chapter 7 can be considered as aspects of the "economic sociology" of class. These include, on different scales, forms of production and labour regimes, social divisions of labour, labour migration, rural-urban divisions and connections, organizational forms of capital and markets, and state policies and practices and their effects. It was suggested that small farmers and classes of labour intersect and are extremely heterogeneous in their composition and characteristics, not least because of the immensely varied ways in which "self-employment" and wage employment can be combined. To paraphrase Lenin (1964a: 33), infinitely diverse combinations of elements of this or that type of labour are possible.

Underlying such heterogeneity is the most pervasive aspect of complexity, which has only been implied so far. As the philosopher Etienne Balibar put it: in a capitalist world, class relations are "*one determining* structure, covering *all* social practices, without being the *only* one" (quoted by Therborn 2007: 88, emphasis in original). In sum, class relations are *universal but not exclusive* "determinations" of social practices in capitalism. They intersect and combine with other social differences and divisions, of which gender is the most widespread and which can also include oppressive and exclusionary relations of race and ethnicity, religion and caste.

These are not social differences and divisions that necessarily originate in capitalism; nor are they necessarily explicable by "the interests of capital." There is an important difference between thinking that whatever exists in the world of capitalism does so because it serves the interests of capital (a "functionalist" explanation) and exploring how what exists is produced as effects of the contradictory dynamics of capitalist social relations — including how they reshape practices and beliefs that predate capitalism. The contradictory dynamics of capitalist social relations also include the unintended consequences of, on one hand, particular paths of accumulation and strategies of political rule by classes of capital and, on the other hand, the pursuit of reproduction by classes of labour and the challenges of "counter-movements" to the rule of capital.

To move from the economic sociology of class relations and dynamics to themes of class identities and consciousness, and from there to the analysis of collective political practice, involves a series of further factors and determinations that affect political agency. First, it is important to emphasize that the economic and social power of capital, rooted in a system of property and commodity relations, has to be secured through its political and ideological rule, exercised — also universally but not exclusively — through the state. We should not assume that the rule of capital works through any simple unity and instrumentality of purpose, nor that it is necessarily coherent in how it seeks to justify itself ideologically as a moral order or in its political strategies and practices. There are no guarantees of unity, coherence and effectiveness in how classes of capital perceive, anticipate, assess, confront and try to contain the social contradictions of capitalism in order both to pursue profit and accumulation and to secure legitimacy for, or at least acquiescence in, how they do so.

Second, a key issue in the political sociology of (fragmented) classes of labour is indicated by Mahmood Mamdani's observation that the "translation" of "social facts" into "political facts" is always contingent and unpredictable (1996: 219). This is especially so because of "the many ways in which power fragment[s] the *circumstances* and *experiences* of the oppressed" (1996: 219, 272, emphasis added). The great variation in *circumstances* was emphasized by the discussion in chapter 7 of patterns of commodification and class formation in the countryside and of the heterogeneity of classes of labour: complexities of the economic sociology of class. For the political sociology of class, a crucial next step is how those circumstances are *experienced*, as Mamdani suggests. Existentially, they are not experienced self-evidently and exclusively as class exploitation and oppression *in general* but in terms of specific identities like "urban/rural dwellers, industrial workers/agricultural labourers, urban craftsmen and women peasants, men/women, mental/manual labour, young/old, black/white, regional, national and ethnic differences, and so on," in the list of examples given by Peter Gibbon and Michael Neocosmos (1985: 190). Moreover, it is common for particular capitals to seize on relational differences — of gender, of generation, of place (town and countryside) and indeed of ethnicity and nationality — in how they recruit labour and organize it in production and in how they deal with resistance from classes of labour.

Barbara Harris-White and Nandini Gooptu (2000: 89) restate a central issue of the political sociology of class thus: "struggle over class" precedes and is a condition of "struggle between classes." In "mapping India's world of unorganized labour," they explore how struggles "over class" by the working poor are inflected and restricted by gender, caste, religious and other social differences and divisions. They conclude that the overwhelming majority of Indian classes of labour "is still engaged in the first struggle," over class, while Indian classes of capital are engaged in the second struggle through their offensives against labour — an argument that can be applied and tested elsewhere, of course.

Class Struggles in the Countryside

There is no doubt that the countrysides of the South are permeated by struggles that manifest the political agency and confrontations of various actors, from agribusiness to national and local classes of landed property and agrarian capital, to different classes of "small" farmers and fragmented classes of labour. All such struggles are shaped universally but not exclusively by class dynamics, which combine in complex ways with structural sources and experiences of other social contradictions. This applies to both different scales and shapes of agency, which I now illustrate briefly.

In terms of "scale," chapter 6 noted the idea of "everyday forms of resistance" in local settings like that of the village. Ben Kerkvliet (2009: 233) emphasizes the continuing relevance of James Scott's approach that "daily life is rife with class struggle that only occasionally bursts into the open." However, such everyday "class struggle" is typically combined with and experienced as oppression rooted in other forms of hierarchy as well. For example, one of the criticisms of Scott's book, *Weapons of the Weak,* is that it is "gender-blind," ignoring the dynamics and effects of unequal gender relations and the agency of women farmers and farm workers (Hart 1991).

As well as "everyday forms of resistance," more overt and intense struggles, sometimes on a larger regional scale, are a feature of widespread conflicts over land in sub-Saharan Africa. Anthropologist Pauline Peters summarizes their class and non-class dynamics, at the same time suggesting how the latter connect with the former:

> Competition over land for different purposes intensifies due to growing populations and movements of people looking for better/more land or fleeing civil disturbances; rural groups seek to intensify commodity production and food production while retrenched members of a downsized salariat look for land to improve food and income options; states demarcate forestry and other reserves, and identify areas worthy of conservation (often under pressure from donors and international lobbying groups); representatives of the state and political elites appropriate land through means ranging from the questionable to the illegal; and valuable resources both on and under the land (timber, oil, gold, other minerals) attract intensifying exploitation by agents from the most local (unemployed youth or erstwhile farmers seeking ways to obtain cash) to transnational networks (of multinational corporations, foreign governments and representatives of African states)....
> [There is] not only intensifying competition over land but deepening social differentiation and, though this differentiation takes many forms — including youth against elders, men against women, ethnic and religious confrontations — these also reveal new social divisions that, in sum, can be seen as class formation.... The proliferating tensions and struggles between generations and genders, or between groups labelled by region, ethnicity or religion, are intimately tied up with the dynamics of division and exclusion, alliance and inclusion that constitute class formation. (2004: 279, 291, 305)

It is striking that the most vicious wars in contemporary sub-Saharan Africa — typically portrayed in the international media as instances of intrinsic African "tribalism" and "barbarism" — have long histories of pressure on and conflicts over land. These conflicts are inflected by the legacies of colonial political and land administration, shaped by patterns of commodification and intensified by the the exploitation of natural resources, climate change and selective intervention by international political actors: for example, in Rwanda and the eastern Congo (Pottier 2002), Sierra Leone and Côte d'Ivoire (Chauveau and Richards 2008) and Darfur (Mamdani 2009). They *are* struggles "between groups labelled by region, ethnicity or religion" but *also* struggles with their own class dynamics, if in "invisible and unarticulated ways" (Peters 1994: 210).

Other instances of usually localized struggles have a more evident class "shape", especially where the recruitment, control and payment of wage labour are concerned. One example is struggles between workers and their employers on capitalist plantations and estates. Another instance is provided by areas of vibrant "peasant capitalism" in India, marked by overt conflict between rich/medium farmers and their workers, who are often subject to systematic violence (Banaji 1990). Both kinds of rural class struggle can be especially fierce when their class dynamics are combined with and compounded by other social differences — divisions of caste and gender in the Indian countryside and of ethnicity in labour recruitment, often a deliberate strategy in plantation labour regimes.

"The People of the Land"

To conclude, I explore issues of organized agrarian movements today — on regional, national and even transnational scales — with particular reference to their "shape" in class and other terms. Are organized agrarian movements today the descendants of the great peasant movements of the past (chapter 6), at least in terms of their scale and significance if not their circumstances and methods, nor perhaps their goals? Eric Wolf's "peasant wars of the twentieth century" were directed against *anciens regimes* of "feudal" provenance, as in Russia and China, and colonial provenance, as in Mexico, Vietnam,

Algeria and Cuba — all of which were subject to pervasive if uneven change as they were incorporated in a capitalist world economy (chapter 3). Such peasant movements mobilized around issues of land, of rent and tax, of pauperization and of extreme oppression and social injustice, often in conditions of generalized social upheaval and war. They were usually part of wider movements of national liberation and social revolution and were all pursued through guerrilla and other warfare. They too had their own marked historical and local specificities and could be heterogeneous in their class composition; for example, a distinctive and much debated element of Wolf's interpretation is his emphasis on the strategic role of "middle peasants" in such movements.

In today's world of neoliberal globalization, there are new types of agrarian movements that, according to those who champion them, aspire to encompass all "small" farmers — or all "small and *medium-scale farmers*" (Desmarais 2007: 6, my emphasis) — in the South and sometimes "family" farmers in the North as well, as an inclusive "people of the land." The political project advocated for this constituency opposes "the corporatization of agriculture... (that) has been globally synchronized to the detriment of farming populations *everywhere*" (McMichael 2006: 473, emphasis added), and proposes to "revaloriz(e) rural cultural-ecology as a global good" by mobilizing a "global agrarian resistance," an "agrarian counter-movement" that strives to preserve or reclaim "the peasant way" — the name of one of the best-known of these movements, *La Vía Campesina*, (472, 474, 480). Whether a global "agrarian counter-movement" actually exists, in what sense, what its impact is and so on, cannot be pursued here.[1] I limit myself to noting the ambition, expressed by Philip McMichael, to forge a unity of all "the people of the land" as, in effect, a single class exploited by corporate capital. This ambition refashions and expands the vision of a long tradition of agrarian populism in current conditions of neoliberal globalization. Any unity of "the people of the land" cannot be assumed , however, but would have to be constructed from heterogeneous local, regional and national "farmers' movements," with all their variations of specific processes of agrarian change and the circumstances of different rural classes (economic sociology), and of specific histories, experiences and cultures of struggle (political sociology). Following are some brief examples.

In Brazil, with its expansive areas of uncultivated private landholdings and which never had a major redistributive agrarian reform, "the land question" has achieved national political significance through the actions of the MST. The MST "invades" and occupies unused lands and establishes farming settlements on them, with an explicitly anti-capitalist ideology of establishing land as common property for those who work it (Introduction, Chapters 2 and 3) while also working closely closely with state agencies to supply funding for infrastructure and new farming enterprises. The political origins, trajectories and culture of the MST include the memory of earlier "peasant leagues" suppressed by military dictatorship in the 1960s, a tradition of radical "social" Catholicism among some priests and church activists, and local alliances with the Workers' Party (currently the party of national government in Brazil). The MST draws on a discourse of class intended to unite all its members, who come from different social locations in the countrysides of Brazil — for example, former plantation workers in the sugar zones of the northeast and small farmers in the south. The experiences they bring with them shape their different expectations and affect the relationship between the organization of community and individual livelihoods, including petty commodity production, in MST settlements, which often diverge from the collective ideal promoted by leaders and admirers of the movement (Wolford, 2003).

If the case of the MST as a national movement illustrates differences among and between specific groups of workers and small farmers, class divisions are more evident in some of the state-wide "new farmers' movements" in India. The Karnataka Rajya Ryota Sangha, (KRRS, Karnataka State Farmers' Association) — a member organization of the international network of La Vía Campesina, has gained wide international recognition for its opposition to genetically modified Bt cotton seed. However, it is run by and for rich and medium farmers, who continue to oppress rural labour and who campaign for subsidies on chemical fertilizers. In short, the social and ecological credentials of the KRRS as an exemplar of "global agrarian resistance" are not as straightforward as it and others claim.

Interestingly, the ideology of "new farmers' movements" in India explicitly points to "people of the city" as the antithesis of "the people of the land," at least in the sense that a strong populist tradition attributes the problems of farmers to "urban bias." Policies are held to favour urban industry — and urban populations more generally, for example, through the supply of "cheap food" — at the expense of farmers. The demands of these movements thus tend to focus on issues of the terms of trade between agricultural and industrial goods (chapters 4 and 6 above). In this respect — their preoccupation with the prices and subsidies farmers receive — they are just like farmers' organizations and lobbies in the E.U. and U.S., and their critics see them as movements dominated by the interests of richer farmers.

Conclusion

I conclude with five final questions, which I adapt from the introductory essay in an important collection, *Transnational Agrarian Movements Confronting Globalization* (Borras et al. 2008), and which apply to all "counter-movements" engaged in agrarian struggles.

1. What are the characteristics of the agrarian structures from which movements emerge, or do not emerge?
2. What is the social basis of agrarian movements? What social classes and groups do they claim to represent? How can the plausibility of such claims be assessed?
3. What issues or demands are put forward by movements? Where do those demands come from, and which social and political forces advance or constrain them?
4. What issues unite and divide agrarian movements, and why?
5. How effective are the actions of those movements in changing the agrarian structures they challenge, and to whose benefit? Why are some movements more effective than others?

To these questions I must add another, concerning the "big picture" with which this book started: how plausible are the claims of agrarian "counter-movements" and their champions that a return to "low-input" small-scale family farming ("re-peasantization") can feed a world population so many times larger, and so much more urban, than the time when "peasants" were the principal producers of the world's food?

The analytical complexities of class dynamics in processes of agrarian change, presented in this short book, represent an attempt to grapple with some of the complexities of the real world of capitalism today. That world extends from the futures exchanges of Chicago and the headquarters of corporate agribusiness through the class differentiation of zones of dynamic "peasant capitalism" to the struggles of the poor farmers and workers pictured in the Introduction. The challenges of complexity are confronted in practice by those activists engaged in trying to build and sustain a progressive politics of agrarian change on its various scales from the most local to the global. To this end, attractive slogans and a list of heroes and villains, good guys and bad guys, are hardly sufficient. Activist movements need an effective analysis of the complex and contradictory social realities they seek to transform. In a capitalist world, understanding class dynamics should always be a point of departure and a central element of such analysis.

Note
1. Edelman (2003) provides a useful survey of such movements.

Glossary

Note: cross-references to terms in this glossary are in italics.

accumulation in capitalism: accumulation of profit to invest in production (or trade, or finance) in order to make more profit; see also *expanded reproduction*

agrarian capital capital invested in farming in order to realize profits

agribusiness corporations on various scales, including global, that invest in agriculture; see also *agri-input and agro-food corporations*

agriculture/agricultural sector in modern *capitalism* farming together with all those economic interests, and their specialized institutions and activities, *upstream* and *downstream* of farming that affect the activities and *reproduction* of farmers

agri-input corporations *agribusiness* corporations that invest in agriculture *upstream* of farming

agro-food corporations *agribusiness* corporations that invest in agriculture *downstream* of farming

biopiracy name given by critics to *agri-input corporations* that try to patent private "intellectual property rights" in genetic plant material

capitalism distinctive socioeconomic system, established on a world scale, that is based in the *class* relation between capital and labour

ceremonial fund part of the *surplus product* used for collective activities in rural communities to mark, e.g., harvests, religious events, or "rites of passage" like marriages and deaths

class the social relation of production between classes of producers (labour) and non-producers; see also *exploitation*

commodification process through which the elements of production and *reproduction* are produced for, and obtained from, market exchange and subjected to its disciplines and compulsions; *capitalism* is distinctive as a system of generalized commodity production

commodification of subsistence process through which key elements of the *subsistence*, hence *reproduction*, of previously "independent"

GLOSSARY

small farmers become subject to the dynamics of market exchange and their compulsions (*commodification*)

commodity chains all the activities that connect the production of commodities with their final consumption; in the case of agricultural commodities the journeys from farmer's field to consumer's plate, and the actors and institutions, relations and practices, that structure those journeys

common property rights rights to land and other resources, e.g. sources of water, grazing and woodland, that are held in common by recognized groups whose members share *usufruct* rights to those resources

consumption fund that part of the product or income required to satisfy the food and other basic needs of producers and their families, including those of *generational reproduction*

depeasantization process by which *peasant* farmers lose access to the means to reproduce themselves as farmers; see also *primitive accumulation, proletarianization, simple reproduction 'squeeze'*

differentiation in class terms the tendency of *petty commodity producers* to divide into classes of capital and labour; also strongly shaped by *gender* relations and their dynamics

domestic labour the activities of cooking, caring for children, and so on, essential to household and social *reproduction* and typically structured by relations of *gender*

"downstream" all those activities concerning agricultural commodities when they leave the farm, such as marketing, processing, wholesale and retail sale, and so on

ecological footprint amount of biologically productive land and sea area, and energy, used by given types of technology to (i) regenerate the resources a human population consumes and (ii) absorb and render harmless the corresponding waste

enclosure process of privatization of land and other resources held as *common property rights*, whether that process happens *de facto* (in practice) or *de jure* (with legal status); see also *"vernacular" markets*

energy productivity the units of energy (calories) used up to produce a quantity of crops of a given energy or calorific value

entry costs the kinds and scale of costs incurred to establish a commodity enterprise, including *"small-scale farming"*

expanded reproduction another name for the *accumulation* of capital, and its investment in expanding the scale of production in order to make more profit; contrasts with *simple reproduction*

exploitation the appropriation of the *surplus product* of classes of producers by (dominant) classes of non-producers

family farmer most robustly applied to farms that use family labour only; sometimes applied to farms that are family owned and/or family managed but not worked with family labour

feudalism "mode of production" in which classes of feudal *landed property* appropriate *surplus produce* from *peasant* producers in the form of rent; see *fund of rent*

financialization process through which finance or money capital becomes dominant over other forms of capital (industrial, mercantile, etc); considered by some as the characteristic tendency of contemporary *globalization*, and manifested in the financial crisis from 2008

fund of rent that part of *surplus product* which *"peasants"* or *"small farmers"* have to pay to others, e.g. landlords, moneylenders, merchants

gender relations between men and women; divisions of property, labour and income are typically structured by unequal gender relations, if in different ways; see also *domestic labour, generational reproduction, social division of labour*

generational reproduction the activities of producing and rearing the next generation; typically structured by *gender* relations

globalization considered, and much debated, as the current phase of world capitalism, especially from the 1970s; marked by largely unregulated international capital markets and *financialization* and by the political project of *neoliberalism*

imperialism conventionally a system of rule of the territories and peoples of other societies/countries by an imperial states; for Lenin the "latest stage" of capitalism, dominated by the most developed capitalist countries and not requiring direct colonial rule

international food regime systems of relations, rules and practices structuring international divisions of labour and trade in agriculture in world capitalism from the 1870s

labour power the capacity to work that workers own as their principal or only commodity and sell for wages in order to buy their means of *reproduction*; uniquely central to the capitalist mode of production

labour process the organization and activities of labour in particular processes of production; see also *technical conditions of production, social conditions of production*

labour productivity the amount of a good (or service) someone can produce with a given expenditure of effort, typically measured or averaged out in terms of time spent working or labour time

labour regime different modes of recruiting/mobilizing labour and organizing it in production

land productivity see *yield*

landed property the class based in effective control of land, whether in precapitalist conditions like *feudalism* or in capitalism with private property rights in land which has been *commodified*

marginal farmers farmers who do not provide the major part of their *reproduction* needs from "own account" farming; an important component of classes of labour; see also *semi-proletarianization*

mercantilism a system of political regulation of trade; the adjective "mercantile" can refer to such a system and, more generically, to the activities of trade and commerce and those who specialize in them (mercantile capital)

monoculture cultivation of extensive areas with a single crop, versus diversified cropping systems

neoliberalism a political and ideological programme to "roll back the state" in the interests of the market and its major capitalist actors

overproduction an intrinsic tendency of capitalist competition and *accumulation* in which more is produced than can be sold to realize the average rate of profit, thereby resulting in "devalorization" of capital invested in production

peasant widely, and often loosely, used to describe "*subsistence*"-oriented "*small*" *farmers* or "*family*" *farmers* in different historical conditions and periods, from precapitalist agrarian civilizations to capitalism today, especially in the South

petty commodity production/producers "small-scale" commodity production in capitalism, combining the class places of capital and labour, whether in a household or an individual; subject to class *differentiation*

primitive accumulation for Marx the historical processes by which the key classes of capitalism are established; for others, processes that continue within established capitalism and rely on often coercive "extra-economic" mechanisms, not least in relation to the *enclosure* of land, forest, water sources etc

production process in which labour is applied in changing nature to satisfy the conditions of human life

productive forces technology and technical culture, including people's capacities to organize themselves to make decisions about production, to carry them out, and to innovate, all of which are shaped by the *social conditions of production*

productivity how much can be produced with a given use of resources; see *energy accounting, labour productivity, yield*

proletarianization process by which classes of labour are formed from previously "independent" farmers, artisan, etc; see also *commodification of subsistence, labour power, primitive accumulation*

repeasantization the process whereby former *marginal farmers, semi-proletarians* or *proletarians* take up farming as a major component of their *reproduction*

reproduction securing the conditions of life and of future production from what is produced or earned now

semi-proletarianization a process of formation of classes of labour who are not completely dispossessed of land and/or other means of *reproduction*, for example, in many rurally based migrant labour systems

sharecropping a practice whereby landowners lease land, and sometimes provide instruments of labour, in return for a share of the crop grown

simple reproduction reproduction at the same level of production and consumption; in effect, *reproduction* without *accumulation*

simple reproduction 'squeeze' process of pressure on the *reproduction* of *petty commodity producers* as either or both capital and labour, associated with the *commodification of subsistence* and often leading to *depeasantization*

small farmer typically refers to farmers whose farm size is determined by the availability of family labour, and sometimes assumed to be oriented to *subsistence* or *simple reproduction*; within this definition farm size varies greatly with type of farming

social conditions of production all those social relations, institutions and practices that shape activities of *production* and *reproduction*, including the *technical conditions of production* and *productive forces*

social division of labour (i) social relations between producers relatively specialized in producing different kinds of goods and services, whose activities are complementary; (ii) activities of different categories of people according to the positions they occupy in particular structures of social relations, notably the *class* relations of capital and labour and *gender* relations

subsistence commonly used to denote satisfying the conditions of *simple reproduction*, in the case of *peasants*, *family farmers* or *small farmers* usually with special reference to their production of food for their own consumption; see *commodification of subsistence*

surplus product what is produced beyond the *simple reproduction* needs of producers, hence representing the product of their "surplus labour"; when appropriated by other classes, the basis of *exploitation*

surplus value the particular form of surplus labour in capitalism; see *surplus product*

technical conditions of production particular sets of *productive forces* organized in *labour processes*, including their *technical division of labour*

technical division of labour the combination of different tasks or *labour processes* performed by workers in a single unit of production, like a factory or a farm

"upstream" all those activities necessary to secure the conditions of farming before it can take place, such as access to land, labour, instruments of labour, and with commodification usually credit as well

usufruct rights the rights of farmers to access to land for cultivation and grazing, forest, water sources, and so on, that are held as *common property*

"vernacular" markets markets in goods and services that are commodities in practice (*de facto*), notably land, in conditions where legally established (*de jure*) private property rights are absent, weak, ambiguous and/or contested

yield (land) measure of the productivity of land: the amount of a crop harvested from a given area of land

References

* signifies recommended further reading of an introductory kind
** signifies recommended further reading of a more advanced kind

Albritton, R. 2009. *Let Them Eat Junk: How Capitalism Creates Hunger and Obesity*. London: Pluto Press.
Amin, S. 1976. *Unequal Development: An Essay on the Social Formations of Peripheral Capitalism*. Hassocks: Harvester Press.
_____. 2003. "World Poverty, Pauperization and Capital Accumulation." *Monthly Review* 55, 5.
Araghi, F. 2009. "The Invisible Hand and the Visible Foot: Peasants, Dispossession and Globalization." In A.H.Akram-Lodhi and C.Kay (eds.), *Peasants and Globalization. Political Economy, Rural Transformation and the Agrarian Question*. London: Routledge.
Arrighi, G. 1994. *The Long Twentieth Century: Money, Power and the Origins of Our Times*. London: Verso.
** Arrighi, G., and J.W. Moore. 2001 "Capitalist Development in World Historical Perspective." In R. Albritton, M. Itoh, R. Westra and A. Zueege (eds.), *Phases of Capitalist Development. Booms, Crises and Globalizations*. London: Palgrave.
Bagchi, A.K. 2009. "Nineteenth Century Imperialism and Structural Transformation in Colonized Countries." In A.H. Akram-Lodhi and C. Kay (eds.), *Peasants and Globalization, Political Economy, Rural Transformation and the Agrarian Question*. London: Routledge.
Banaji, J. 1990. "Illusions about the Peasantry: Karl Kautsky and the Agrarian Question." *Journal of Peasant Studies* 17, 2.
_____. 1997. "Modernizing the Historiography of Rural Labour: An Unwritten Agenda." In M. Bentley (ed.), *Companion to Historiography*. London: Routledge.
_____. 2002. "The Metamorphoses of Agrarian Capitalism." *Journal of Agrarian Change* 2, 1.
_____. 2007. "Islam, the Mediterranean and the Rise of Capitalism." *Historical Materialism* 15, 1.
_____. 2010. *Theory as History: Essays on Modes of Production and Exploitation*. Leiden: Brill.
Barker, J. 1989. *Rural Communities in Distress. Peasant Farmers and the State in Africa*. Cambridge: Cambridge University Press.
Bauer, A.J. 1979. "Rural Workers in Spanish America: Problems of Peonage and Oppression." *Hispanic American Historical Review* 59, 1.

Bello, W. 2009. *The Food Wars*. London: Verso.
Bernstein, H. 1981. "Notes on State and Peasantry." *Review of African Political Economy* 21.
Bharadwaj, K. 1985. "A View of Commercialisation in Indian Agriculture and the Development of Capitalism." *Journal of Peasant Studies* 12, 4.
** Borras, S.M., M. Edelman and C. Kay. 2008. "Transantional Agrarian Movements: Origins and Politics, Campaigns and Impact." In S.M. Borras, M. Edelman and C. Kay (eds.), *Transnational Agrarian Movements Confronting Globalization*. Special issue of *Journal of Agrarian Change* 8, 1-2.
Bray, F. 1986. *The Rice Economies. Technology and Development in Asian Societies*. Oxford: Basil Blackwell.
Breman, J. 1996. *Footloose Labour. Working in India's Informal Economy*. Cambridge: Cambridge University Press.
Brenner, R.P. 2001 "The Low Countries in the Transition to Capitalism." *Journal of Agrarian Change* 1, 2.
Bryceson, D. 1999. "African Rural Labour, Income Diversification and Livelihood Approaches: A Long-term Development Perspective." *Review of African Political Economy* 80.
Burch, D. 2003. "Production, Consumption and Trade in Poultry." In N. Fold and B. Pritchard (eds.), *Cross-continental Food Chains*. London: Routledge.
Byres T.J. 1981. "The New Technology, Class Formation and Class Action in the Indian Countryside." *Journal of Peasant Studies* 8, 4.
_____. 1991. "The Agrarian Question and Differing Forms of Capitalist Transition: An Essay with Reference to Asia." In J. Breman and S. Mundle (eds.), *Rural Transformation in Asia*. Delhi: Oxford University Press.
_____. 1996. *Capitalism From Above and Capitalism From Below: An Essay in Comparative Political Economy*. London: Macmillan.
Chauveau, J-P, and P. Richards. 2008. "West African Insurgencies in Agrarian Perspective: Côte d'Ivoire amd Sierra Leone Compared." *Journal of Agrarian Change* 8, 4.
Chayanov, A.V. 1966 [1925]. *The Theory of Peasant Economy*. D. Thorner, B. Kerblay and R.E.F. Smith (eds.). Homewood, IL: Richard Irwin for the American Economic Association.
_____. 1991 [1927]. *The Theory of Peasant Co-operatives*. London: I.B. Tauris.
** Chimhowu, A., and P. Woodhouse. 2007. "Customary vs Private Property Rights? Dynamics and Trajectories of Vernacular Land Markets in

Sub-Saharan Africa." *Journal of Agrarian Change* 6, 3.
Chonchol, J. 1970, "Eight Fundamental Conditions of Agrarian Reform in Latin America." In R. Stavenhagen (ed.), *Agrarian Problems and Peasant Movements in Latin America*. New York: Doubleday.
Cordell, D., J.W. Gregory and V. Piché. 1996. *Hoe and Wage: A Social History of a Circular Migration System in West Africa*, Boulder, CO: Westview Press.
Cowen, M.P., and R.W. Shenton. 1991a. "The Origin and Course of Fabian Colonialism in Africa." *Journal of Historical Sociology* 4, 2.
_____. 1991b. "Bankers, Peasants and Land in British West Africa, 1905–1937." *Journal of Peasant Studies* 19, 1.
** Cronon, W. 1991. *Nature's Metropolis. Chicago and the Great West*. New York: W.W. Norton.
** Crosby, A.W. 1986. *Ecological Imperialism: The Biological Expansion of Europe 900–1900*. Cambridge: Cambridge University Press.
Daviron, B. 2002. "Small Farm Production and the Standardization of Tropical Products." *Journal of Agrarian Change* 2, 2.
Davis, M. 2001. *Late Victorian Holocausts. El Niño Famines and the Making of the Third World*. London: Verso.
** _____. 2006. *Planet of Slums*. London: Verso.
Desmarais, A.A. 2007. *La Vía Campesina: Globalization and the Power of Peasants*. Halifax: Fernwood Publishing.
Djurfeldt, G. 1981. "What Happened to the Agrarian Bourgeoisie and Rural Proletariat Under Monopoly Capitalism? Some Hypotheses Derived from the Classics of Marxism on the Agrarian Question." *Acta Sociologica* 24, 3.
Duncan, C.A.M. 1996. *The Centrality of Agriculture. Between Humanity and the Rest of Nature*. Montreal: McGill-Queen's University Press.
Edelman, M. 1999. *Peasants Against Globalization: Rural Social Movements in Costa Rica*. Stanford: Stanford University Press.
** _____. 2003. "Transnational Peasant and Farmer Movements and Networks." In M. Kaldor, H. Anheier and M. Glasius (eds.), *Global Civil Society Yearbook 2003*. London: Sage.
Ellis, F. 1999. "Household Strategies and Rural Livelihood Diversification." *Journal of Development Studies* 35, 1.
Francks, P. 2006. *Rural Economic Development in Japan from the Nineteenth Century to the Pacific War*. London: Routledge.
Frank, A.G. 1967. *Capitalism and Underdevelopment in Latin America*. New York: Monthly Review Press.
* Friedmann, H. 1990 "The Origins of Third World Food Dependence." In

H. Bernstein, B. Crow, M. Mackintosh and C. Martin (eds.), *The Food Question*. London: Earthscan and New York: Monthly Review Press.

_____. 1993. "The Political Economy of Food: A Global Crisis." *New Left Review* 197.

** _____. 2004. "Feeding the Empire: The Pathologies of Globalized Agriculture." In L. Panitch and C. Leys (eds.), *The Socialist Register 2005*. London: Merlin Press.

_____. 2006. "Focusing on Agriculture: A Comment on Henry Bernstein's 'Is There an Agrarian Question in the 21st Century?'" *Canadian Journal of Development Studies* 27, 4.

Friedmann, H., and P. McMichael. 1989. "Agriculture and the State System: The Rise and Decline of National Agricultures, 1870 to the Present." *Sociologica Ruralis* 29, 2.

Gibbon, P. and M. Neocosmos. 1985. "Some Problems in the Political Economy of 'African Socialism.'" In H. Bernstein and B.K. Campbell (eds.), *Contradictions of Accumulation in Africa: Studies in Economy and State*. Beverly Hills, CA: Sage.

Gilsenan, M. 1982. *Recognizing Islam*. London: Croom Helm.

Goody, J. 2004. *Capitalism and Modernity: The Great Debate*. Cambridge: Polity Press.

Grigg, D.B. 1974. *The Agrarian Systems of the World: An Evolutionary Approach*. Cambridge: Cambridge University Press.

Harriss, J. 1987. "Capitalism and Peasant Production the Green Revolution in India." In T. Shanin (ed.), *Peasants and Peasant Societies*. Second edition. Oxford: Blackwell.

Harriss-White, B., and N. Gooptu. 2000. "Mapping India's World of Unorganized Labour." In L. Panitch and C. Leys (eds.), *The Socialist Register 2001*. London: Merlin Press.

Hart, G. 1991. "Engendering Everyday Resistance: Gender, Patronage and Production Politics in Rural Malaysia." *Journal of Peasant Studies* 19, 1.

_____. 1994. "The Dynamics of Diversification in an Asian Rice Region." In B. Koppel, J.N. Hawkins and W. James (eds.), *Development or Deterioration? Work in Rural Asia*. Boulder, CO: Lynne Reinner.

* Hartmann, B., and J.K. Boyce. 1983. *A Quiet Violence. View from a Bangladesh Village*. London: Zed Books.

Harvey, D. 2005. *A Brief History of Neoliberalism*. Oxford: Oxford University Press.

Hazell, P., C. Poulton, S. Wiggins, and A. Dorward. 2007. *The Future of Small Farms for Poverty Reduction and Growth*. Washington: IFPRI (International Food Policy Research Institute). 2020 Discussion

Paper 42.

Hilferding, R. 1981 [1910]. *Finance Capital*. London: Routledge & Kegan Paul.

Hill, P. 1963. *The Migrant Cocoa Farmers of Southern Ghana*. Cambridge: Cambridge University Press.

IFAD 2001. *Rural Poverty Report 2001: The Challenge of Ending Rural Poverty*. Rome: International Fund for Agricultural Development.

Kautsky, K. 1988 [1899]. *The Agrarian Question*. Two volumes. P. Burgess trans. London: Zwan.

Kay, C. 1974. "Comparative Development of the European Manorial System and the Latin American Hacienda System." *Journal of Peasant Studies*, 2, 1.

Kay, G. 1975. *Development and Underdevelopment*. London: Macmillan.

Kerkvliet, B.J. Tria. 2009. "Everyday Politics in Peasant Societies (and Ours)." *Journal of Peasant Studies* 36, 1.

* Kitching, G. 1982. *Development and Underdevelopment in Historical Perspective*. London: Methuen.

** _____. 2001. *Seeking Social Justice through Globalization*, University Park, PA: Pennsylvania State University Press.

** Kloppenburg Jr, J.R. 2004. *First the Seed. The Political Economy of Plant Biotechnology*. Second edition. Madison: University of Wisconsin Press.

Koning, N. 1994. *The Failure of Agrarian Capitalism: Agrarian Politics in the United Kingdom, Germany, the Netherlands and the USA, 1846–1919*. London: Routledge.

Lenin, V.I. 1964a [1899]. *The Development of Capitalism in Russia: The Process of the Formation of a Home Market for Large-Scale Industry*. In *Collected Works* Volume 3, Moscow: Progress Publishers.

_____. 1964b [1916]. *Imperialism, The Highest Stage of Capitalism*. In *Collected Works* Volume 22, Moscow: Progress Publishers.

Low, D.A. 1996. *The Egalitarian Moment: Asia and Africa 1950–1980*. Cambridge: Cambridge University Press.

Mamdani, M. 1987. "Extreme but not Exceptional: Towards an Analysis of the Agrarian Question in Uganda." *Journal of Peasant Studies* 14, 2.

_____. 1996. *Citizen and Subject: Contemporary Africa and the Legacy of Late Colonialism*. Cape Town: David Philip.

_____. 2009. *Saviors and Survivors: Darfur, Politics and the War on Terror*. London: Verso.

Mann, S.A., and J.M. Dickinson. 1978. "Obstacles to the Development of a Capitalist Agriculture." *Journal of Peasant Studies* 5,4.

Martinez-Alier, J. 2002. *The Environmentalism of the Poor*. Cheltenham:

Edward Elgar.

Marx, K. 1973. *Grundrisse: Foundations of the Critique of Political Economy (Rough Draft)*. Harmondsworth: Penguin (from Marx's notebooks of 1857–8; Martin Nicolaus, trans.).

_____. 1976 [1867]. *Capital*. Volume I. Ben Fowkes, trans. Harmondsworth: Penguin.

* Mazoyer, M. and L. Roudart. 2006. *A History of World Agriculture from the Neolithic Age to the Current Crisis*. London: Earthscan.

Mbilinyi, M. 1990 "Structural Adjustment, Agribusiness and Rural Women in Tanzania." In H. Bernstein, B. Crow, M. Mackintosh and C. Martin (eds.), *The Food Question*. London: Earthscan and New York: Monthly Review Press.

McMichael, P. 2006. "Reframing Development: Global Peasant Movements and the New Agrarian Question." *Canadian Journal of Development Studies* 27,4.

Mendes, C. 1992. "The Defence of Life." *Journal of Peasant Studies* 20, 1.

Moore Jr., Barrington. 1966. *Social Origins of Dictatorship and Democracy: Lord and Peasant in the Making of the Modern World*. Boston: Beacon Press.

Moore J.W. 2003. "*The Modern World-System* as Environmental History? Ecology and the Rise of Capitalism." *Theory & Society* 32, 3.

_____. 2010a. "'Amsterdam is Standing on Norway'. Part I: The Alchemy of Capital, Empire, and Nature in the Diaspora of Silver, 1545–1648." *Journal of Agrarian Change* 10, 1.

_____. 2010b. "'Amsterdam is Standing on Norway'. Part II: The Global North Atlantic in the Ecological Revolution of Seventeenth Century Capitalism." *Journal of Agrarian Change* 10, 2.

Myrdal, G. 1968. *Asian Drama: An Inquiry into the Poverty of Nations*. Three volumes. New York: Pantheon Books.

Panitch, L., and C. Leys. 2000. "Preface." In L. Panitch and C. Leys (eds.), *The Socialist Register 2001*. London: Merlin Press.

Patel, Raj. 2007. *Stuffed and Starved: Markets, Power and the Hidden Battle for the World's Food System*. London: Portobello Books.

Peters, P.E. 1994. *Dividing the Commons: Politics, Policy and Culture in Botswana*. Charlottesville: University of Virginia Press.

** _____. 2004. "Inequality and Social Conflict over Land in Africa." *Journal of Agrarian Change* 4, 3.

Polanyi, K., 1957 [1944]. *The Great Transformation: The Political and Economic Origin of Our Time*. Boston: Beacon Press.

Pomeranz, K. 2000. *The Great Divergence: China, Europe and the Making of the Modern World Economy*. Princeton: Princeton University Press.

Post, C. 1995. "The Agrarian Origins of US Capitalism: The Transformation of the Northern Countryside Before the Civil War." *Journal of Peasant Studies* 22, 3.

Pottier, J. 2002. *Re-Imagining Rwanda: Conflict, Survival and Disinformation in the Late Twentieth Century*. Cambridge: Cambridge University Press.

Preobrazhensky, E. 1965 [1926]. *The New Economics*. Brian Pearce, trans. Oxford: Clarendon Press.

Richards, P. 1986. *Coping with Hunger: Hazard and Experiment in an African Rice Farming System*. London: Allen & Unwin.

Sahlins, M. 1972. *Stone Age Economics*. Chicago: Aldine.

Schwartz, H.M. 2000. *States versus Markets: The Emergence of A Global Economy*. Second edition. Houndmills, Basingstoke: Palgrave.

Scott, J.C. 1985. *Weapons of the Weak: Everyday Forms of Peasant Resistance*. New Haven: Yale University Press.

_____. 2005. "Afterword to 'Moral Economies, State Spaces, and Categorical Violence.'" *American Anthropologist* 107, 3.

Sen, A. 1981. *Poverty and Famines*. Oxford: Oxford University Press.

Sender, J., and S. Smith. 1986. *The Development of Capitalism in Africa*. London: Methuen.

Shanin, T. 1986. "Chayanov's Message: Illuminations, Miscomprehensions, and the Contemporary 'Development Theory.'" In A.V. Chayanov, D. Thorner, B. Kerblay and R.E.F. Smith (eds.), *The Theory of Peasant Economy*. Second edition. Madison: University of Wisconsin Press.

Shelley, T. 2007. *Exploited: Migrant Labour in the New Global Economy*. London: Zed Books.

Silver, B.J., and G. Arrighi. 2000. "Workers North and South." In L. Panitch and C. Leys (eds.), *The Socialist Register 2001*. London: Merlin Press.

Stolcke, V., and M.M. Hall. 1983. "The Introduction of Free Labour on São Paulo Coffee Plantations." *Journal of Peasant Studies* 10, 2/3.

Stoler, A. 1985. *Capitalism and Confrontation in Sumatra's Plantation Belt, 1870–1979*. New Haven: Yale University Press.

Striffler, S. 2004. "Class Formation in Latin America: One Family's Enduring Journey between Country and City." *International Labor and Working-Class History* 65.

Therborn, G. 2007. "After Dialectics: Radical Social Theory in a Post-Communist World." *New Left Review* (NS) 43.

** van der Ploeg, J.D. 2008. *The New Peasantries: Struggles for Autonomy and Sustainability in an Era of Empire and Globalization*. London: Earthscan.

von Freyhold, M. 1979. *Ujamaa Villages in Tanzania: Analysis of a Social*

Experiment. London: Heinemann.

Wallerstein, I. 1979. *The Capitalist World-Economy*. Cambridge: Cambridge University Press.

Warren, B. 1980. *Imperialism: Pioneer of Capitalism*. London: Verso.

* Weis, T. 2007. *The Global Food Economy: The Battle for the Future of Farming*. London: Zed Books.

Whitcombe, E. 1980. "Whatever Happened to the Zamindars?" In E.J. Hobsbawm, W. Kula, A. Mitra, K.N. Raj and I. Sachs (eds.), *Peasants in History: Essays in Honour of Daniel Thorner*. Calcutta: Oxford University Press.

Williams, G. 1976. "Taking the Part of Peasants." In P. Gutkind and I. Wallerstein (eds.), *The Political Economy of Contemporary Africa*. Beverly Hills, CA: Sage.

* Wolf, E. 1966. *Peasants*. Englewood Cliffs, NJ: Prentice Hall.

** _____. 1969. *Peasant Wars of the Twentieth Century*. New York: Harper and Row.

Wolford, W. 2003. "Producing Community: The MST and Land Reform Settlements in Brazil." *Journal of Agrarian Change* 3, 4.

Wood, E. Meiksins. 2003. *Empire of Capital*. London: Verso.

World Bank. 2007. *World Development Report 2008: Agriculture for Development*. Washington: World Bank.

Index

accumulation 1, 9, 20, 22-25, 27, 32, 33, 35, 40, 42, 53, 57, 58, 63, 80, 84, 86, 87, 95, 101, 107, 116
   primitive 27, 28, 30, 32, 36, 56-7, 58, 77, 87, 95, 102
   regimes ("regimes of accumulation") 35
Africa 2, 14, 16, 36, 39-43, 46, 48, 52-8, 68-71, 73, 74, 96, 97, 100, 104, 109, 113, 118, 119
   North 1, 21, 63, 73, 107
   sub-Saharan 2, 14, 15, 41, 50-2, 75, 96, 107-108, 118, 119,
   West 36, 40
agrarian transition 27-32, 55, 57
agribusiness 47, 67, 68, 74, 79, 81, 83, 86, 112, 117, 123
agricultural modernization 73-76, 99
agricultural sector 61, 62, 64, 65, 75, 110
Argentina 24, 42, 44, 46, 47, 66, 81
agro-food industry 65, 72, 73, 81, 82, 84, 89, 90, 92, 94, 95, 110
Algeria 96, 98, 120
Asia 1, 21, 28, 30, 32, 39-45, 47, 52-55, 57, 58, 63, 68-71, 73, 74, 100, 104, 107, 109

Bolivia 46, 98
Brazil 2, 5, 7-9, 24, 39, 40, 43, 44, 46, 47, 54, 66, 78, 81, 100, 121

capitalist farming 4, 5, 6, 27-32, 35, 37, 47, 51, 55, 59, 61, 65-8, 71, 76, 77, 85, 89-101, 104-106, 110, 117
Caribbean 39, 40, 44, 52-4, 66, 87, 107
Central America 21, 44, 46, 47, 52, 63
class
   differentiation 4, 29, 31, 50, 103, 104-110, 123
   sociology of 88, 112, 115-117
   struggles 100, 117-119
   violence 9, 119,
Chile 24, 44, 46, 47, 78, 99
China 2, 49, 60, 81, 83, 96, 98, 100, 119
colonialism 36, 39-60, 63, 64, 68, 73, 96, 97, 108
   legacies 8, 46, 119
commodity
   production 4, 25, 27-9, 31, 33, 34, 50-2, 54, 55, 69, 85, 92, 93, 97, 100, 102-104, 106, 109-112, 118, 121
   relations 75, 84, 100, 102, 103, 108, 116
commodification 23, 28, 29, 50, 80, 85, 95-7, 102-103, 105, 108-110, 116, 119
   of subsistence 4, 34, 49, 53, 55, 65, 69, 87, 97, 102, 104
community 3, 20, 28, 97, 121
Corn Laws 69, 73, 87
corporate agriculture 11, 72, 81, 85, 87, 88, 112, 123
Cuba 44, 46, 96, 98, 120

debt 45-6, 49, 54, 84, 96, 104, 105, 108,
dispossession 28, 30, 32, 34, 35,

44, 46, 50, 55, 87, 89, 95, 96, 101
economic
  activity 15, 22, 24, 79, 107
  development 53, 57-9, 65, 76, 80, 86, 96, 97
Ecuador 5, 6, 8
Egypt 34, 63, 99, 100
England 9, 27-9, 30, 31, 33, 35, 37, 39, 55, 57, 60, 64, 66, 77, 87, 100, 102
environment 8, 13, 15, 16, 76, 82, 83, 89, 91
Europe 1, 2, 9, 21, 27, 28, 29, 34, 36, 37, 39- 42, 44-6, 48, 51, 55-8, 60, 64, 67-70, 72, 77, 81, 83, 85, 86, 98, 106, 107
exploitation 9, 20-2, 26, 27, 33, 36, 49, 51, 57, 58, 87, 92-5, 101, 116, 118, 119
  self- 94, 101
exports 7, 8, 24, 32, 40, 42, 46-50, 52, 53, 58, 66-70, 72, 74, 76, 85
extra-economic coercion 54, 55

famine 49, 71, 109
farm
  family 3, 4, 31, 32, 85, 86, 88, 89, 91-5, 101, 102, 105, 109, 110, 112, 120, 122
  inputs 6, 8, 15, 65, 73, 75, 122
  marginal 3, 46, 54, 105, 107, 109-111
  medium 85, 104, 105, 107-9, 119-121
  small-scale 3, 4, 7, 8, 11, 23, 28, 29, 31, 33, 45, 47, 59, 71, 77, 82, 84, 85, 87-9, 91, 92, 94-106, 108, 109, 111-113, 115, 117, 120-122
farm size 4, 7, 61, 71, 93, 105

feudalism 27-9, 31, 39, 44
food regime 86, 87
  first 66-70
  second 71-3, 81-2
forests 6, 7, 33, 37, 49, 50, 52, 68, 69, 118
forced commercialization 49, 51, 55, 102
free trade 69, 70-1
fund
  ceremonial 20, 21
  consumption 18, 20, 103, 106
  of rent 20, 21, 49, 103
  replacement 18-20, 103

gender 7-9, 19, 20, 63, 103, 106, 115, 117-119,
  violence 9
Ghana 51, 97
globalization 42, 59, 76, 77, 79-88, 96, 101, 108, 120,
Green Revolution 6, 7, 73, 74, 76, 78, 105

hacienda 8, 34, 44-6, 59
history 2, 8, 10, 11, 19, 23, 27, 33, 35-7, 51, 60, 64, 65, 67, 86, 87, 91, 98
household 3, 7, 19, 20, 24, 55, 63, 64, 73, 78, 93-5, 103, 104, 106, 108, 109, 112

incorporation 48, 52, 53, 58, 67, 68, 93, 120
immigration 42, 44, 46, 69
imperialism 42-3
  ecological 63
India 2, 3, 5-7, 14, 16, 40, 41, 46, 47, 49- 51, 53, 54, 56, 60, 64, 70, 73-6, 83, 84, 96, 99, 100, 105, 108, 109, 117, 119, 121, 122

indigenous peoples 32, 39, 44-50, 58, 70, 96
Indonesia 52
industrialization 2, 9, 27, 30, 32, 36, 37, 41, 52, 58, 65, 71, 73, 76, 77, 83, 85, 90, 91
investment 25, 26, 31, 32, 41, 75, 77, 81, 84, 88, 89, 106, 110
Iran 99, 100

Japan 14, 30, 32, 37, 41, 48, 60, 98, 100

Kenya 34, 51

La Vía Campesina 47, 120, 121
labour 1, 2, 4, 5, 7, 8, 13- 20, 21, 22, 25, 26- 36, 39-41, 43-6, 48, 50-52, 58, 61, 63, 65, 67-9, 71, 77, 80, 84, 87, 89-90, 91-5, 96, 97, 101-112, 115-117, 119, 121
  domestic 19-20
  family 4, 93, 94, 101, 104, 107,
  landless 28, 34
  productivity 13-17, 20, 58, 66, 71, 77, 94,
  regime 34, 45, 53- 8, 115, 119,
  social division 16-17, 20, 23-4, 61, 63-5, 69, 111, 115,
  technical division 17
  wage 4, 31, 34, 35, 45, 46, 69, 91, 93, 94, 102, 104, 106, 107, 109, 112, 119
  surplus 26
  exploitation 33, 34, 59
land
  enclosure 29-31, 48, 91, 87, 88, 102
  expropriation 48, 50,
  output 13, 15, 49, 95,
  reform 32, 74, 97, 98-100, 121

Landless Workers Movement 47
landlord 21, 27, 28, 31, 32, 37, 45, 47, 48, 50, 60, 108,
Latin America 4, 8, 29, 34, 37, 39, 41, 44-8, 53-5, 58-60, 73, 74, 85, 96, 98, 99, 104, 107
Lenin 29-31, 41-3, 104, 111, 115
Lesotho 51
livelihood 2, 3, 6-8, 46, 110, 111, 121,
  diversification 106

Malawi 51
Malaysia 53, 96
markets 3, 4, 7, 8, 25, 27, 33, 34, 40-2, 45, 46, 49-53, 58, 61, 62, 64, 65, 67, 70, 75-7, 79, 80-3, 85, 92, 95, 99, 100, 102, 103, 106, 111, 115
Marx 9-11, 13, 16-19, 25, 26, 29, 32, 33-35, 55-7, 59, 60, 64, 65, 71, 86, 94, 102, 104, 109
Mexico 2, 34, 39, 46, 63, 96, 98, 119
mining 33, 37, 41, 51, 69, 76
Mozambique 51, 98

"national development" 65, 73, 85, 86, 97
nature 13-16, 18-21, 66-70, 80, 89-91
neoliberalism 79-88, 96, 108, 111, 120
Nicaragua 98
North America 39, 40, 44, 48, 77, 85, 86, 92, 94

overproduction 71, 77, 80, 81, 82

Peru 34, 39, 46, 98
petty commodity production 4, 31, 53, 54, 92, 102-106,

109-112, 121,
plantations 31, 34, 39-41, 44, 46, 48, 51-53, 66, 98, 119, 121,
   industrial 52, 68, 69,
Polanyi 100, 102
political economy 1-11, 16, 22-24, 95, 101
Portugal 39, 41, 43, 57
poverty 8, 16, 49, 78, 98, 107
pre-capitalist society 4, 27, 29, 36, 55, 56, 59, 60
privatization 6, 7, 23, 28, 74, 80, 81, 84, 97, 102, 103
property rights 28, 47, 48, 50, 83, 98, 99, 102
Prussia 29-31

reproduction 1, 3, 18-26, 33, 65, 83, 86, 89, 94, 95, 101-111, 116
resistance 89, 95-101, 109, 117
   everyday forms of 117, 118
   global agrarian 120, 121
Russia (also U.S.S.R.; Soviet Union) 30, 56, 60, 71, 81, 86, 87, 92, 96, 98, 119

slavery 5, 21, 26, 27, 31, 34, 39-41, 44, 46, 53, 54, 56, 66, 100
social
   conditions 16, 18, 19, 27, 63,
   differentiation 20, 34, 52, 96, 118
   divisions 4, 16, 17, 20, 23-4, 61, 63-5, 69, 111, 115, 117, 118
   movements 47, 88, 89, 95, 98,
   production 23, 24, 91, 101, 102
   relations 1, 8, 18-24, 26, 46, 57-9, 61, 63, 101, 102, 112, 115-116
South Africa 34, 41, 51, 53
South America 52, 68, 77

South Korea 30, 32
Spain 39, 41, 57
subsistence 1, 3, 4, 20, 26, 28, 29, 33, 34, 43-6, 49, 51-53, 55, 65, 69, 87, 96, 97, 101-104
surplus 4, 20-3, 45, 48, 50, 58, 70
   food 72, 81
   labour 21, 22, 23, 26
   Value 26, 36
state-led development 74, 80, 84, 86

Tanzania 5, 7-9, 75, 103
taxation 21, 22, 30, 32, 37, 47-9, 51, 54, 56, 64, 65, 96, 120
technology 4, 8, 14-16, 18, 105
tenancy 28, 31, 32, 34, 45, 48, 52

Uganda 109
underdevelopment 56, 58
urban 2, 21, 52, 67, 87, 91, 106, 108, 110, 111, 113, 115-117, 122, 123
Uruguay 24, 44, 46, 47, 82
usufruct rights 6-7
U.S. (America) 14, 16, 29-31, 35, 37, 40, 42, 54, 56, 57, 63, 68, 77, 93, 100

Vietnam 74, 87, 96, 98, 119

World Bank 74, 84, 107

Zambia 51
Zimbabwe 51